"We're Going to Have to Let You Go *outlines the most critical part of being successful in business; companies need great people to stay great and keep growing. Isaac also touches on one of the most overlooked costs in business, keeping people around with the wrong attitudes and non-performing employees.* We're Going to Have to Let You Go *gives great insight on how to address these challenges and see them as opportunities to make teams and companies stronger."*

—**Chad Angeli,** international sales director
for a publically traded company on the NYSE

*"As an employment attorney, I recommend that business owners read this book before they call their attorney. It will save them money."*

—**Shannon Sperry,** Seattle attorney

*"As a business owner who has learned the hard way about hiring and keeping the wrong people, I have found* We are going to have to let you go *to be a MUST read for anyone making hiring decisions."*

—**Raymon Kooner,** entrepreneur

WE'RE GOING TO HAVE TO

# LET YOU GO

WE'RE GOING TO HAVE TO

# LET YOU GO

A Guide for Effectively–and
Professionally–Terminating Employees

## ISAAC HAMMER

Published by Advantage, Charleston, South Carolina.
Member of Advantage Media Group.

ADVANTAGE is a registered trademark and the Advantage colophon is a trademark of Advantage Media Group, Inc.

Printed in the United States of America.

ISBN: 978-1-59932-605-4
LCCN: 2015947975

This publication is designed to provide accurate and authoritative information in regard to the subject matter covered. It is sold with the understanding that the publisher is not engaged in rendering legal, accounting, or other professional services. If legal advice or other expert assistance is required, the services of a competent professional person should be sought.

 Advantage Media Group is proud to be a part of the Tree Neutral® program. Tree Neutral offsets the number of trees consumed in the production and printing of this book by taking proactive steps such as planting trees in direct proportion to the number of trees used to print books. To learn more about Tree Neutral, please visit www.treeneutral.com. To learn more about Advantage's commitment to being a responsible steward of the environment, please visit www.advantagefamily.com/green

Advantage Media Group is a publisher of business, self-improvement, and professional development books and online learning. We help entrepreneurs, business leaders, and professionals share their Stories, Passion, and Knowledge to help others Learn & Grow. Do you have a manuscript or book idea that you would like us to consider for publishing? Please visit advantagefamily.com or call 1.866.775.1696.

# TABLE OF CONTENTS

# INTRODUCTION

As a business owner, I spend the majority of my time solving problems. Terminating an employee can be one of the most draining and time-consuming problems that I, and every other business owner, face. That is why I wrote this book, because terminating an employee effectively gives me the freedom to focus on growing my company and becoming more successful.

## MY BACKGROUND

I grew up in Minneapolis, right in the city. I went to a big-city public high school. It wasn't a terrible school, but I wasn't a good student. So I ended up going to community college. I went to Normandale Community College in the Twin Cities area for two years before my grades were good enough to transfer to a four-year college. Then I transferred to the University of Wisconsin-Milwaukee where I graduated in December 2000 with a bachelor of arts degree.

In the fall of 2000, before I graduated, I started to apply to law schools. However, between October 2000 and March 2001, each school either rejected my application or simply did not respond.

One of these was a small law school—William Mitchell College of Law in St. Paul. My aunt went there, and it was in my hometown. I really wanted to be admitted, but I had not been accepted. Meanwhile, the pressure around me was mounting, as most of my friends were either being admitted to graduate programs of their own or were being offered jobs to begin their chosen career. My confidence started to waiver, and I began to question what my career was going to be.

For Easter weekend, I visited my parents back in the Twin Cities. During the trip, I put on a suit and tie, and without an appointment, I walked into the dean's office at William Mitchell. The dean didn't know me, but I asked to speak to him anyway. I told him who I was and that I had applied to the school, but I had not been accepted, and I didn't know why. I told him I wanted to go to school there and that they were making a mistake by not letting me in.

He gave me a strange look, which let me know I had caught him off guard. He took me to the dean of admissions, who was kind enough to pull my file and give me some attention even though I had not made an appointment. He was really candid with me. He said my grades were pretty good, but my writing—a big strength for attorneys—was poor. In fact, that was one of the biggest skills they considered.

He challenged me to write an essay on how I would improve my writing and to also have one of my college professors write him a letter explaining how I had improved my writing skills while I was at college—a somewhat daunting task. I had to tuck my tail a little bit, swallow my pride, and go back to a professor and ask for a favor.

Instead of getting angry or defensive, I felt like I was challenged. I knew what I had to do. I wrote the essay, obtained the letter from my professor, and was accepted into William Mitchell College of Law.

Even though I struggled to get in, I ended up working hard while I was there and ultimately became a pretty good student. I met my wife, Karen, there, and she and I moved out to the Seattle area in the spring of 2004 after we graduated. Our plan was to pass the bar, become attorneys in the Seattle area, and start a new life on the West Coast.

However, in October 2004, I failed the bar exam. This meant six more months of waiting tables and clerking at temp jobs. My confidence was low again.

I retook the exam in February 2005. I remember sitting in my room studying the night before. For a break I turned on the TV and started watching a legal drama. I remember wondering if I would ever realize my dream of becoming an attorney. My resolve to succeed and get better is what truly got me through it. I studied much harder this time, and when I saw the questions, I knew I was prepared. This was a lesson for me. Preparation will provide certainty, and certainty will provide courage to get the job done. I passed the bar.

After months of searching for a job, Karen convinced the attorney she was working for to hire me as an associate. Finally, my first attorney job! With one other associate we made a four-attorney firm that had fewer than 30 employees.

Two years later, the attorney-owner of the firm asked Karen and me to buy him out, a deal that we signed and completed in the spring of 2008. At that time, we were a firm of five attorneys and 29 employees. Since then, Karen and I have grown the firm into a seven-state practice with 15 attorneys and 110 employees.

We are a creditor's rights law firm, whose clients include several Fortune 500 companies. We've grown through acquisition and by taking advantage of opportunities in other markets. But with all of that growth, I have been faced with the challenge of terminating many employees. I have experienced a variety of reasons for an employee no longer being a good fit: employees who can no longer keep up with the speed of the work; employees with bad attitudes;

employees who do not catch on to the training; and a multitude of other reasons.

Over time, I've developed a system that I believe in and that has helped me overcome the emotional hesitancy of deciding to let somebody go in an effective and professional way. That's why I wanted to write this book.

## ENTREPRENEURS HATE FIRING PEOPLE

Most of the entrepreneurs that I meet hate firing people. And with good reason. Most entrepreneurs either self-start their own company or they buy a really small business that has no human resources department. Either way, they usually have no training or coaching from someone who has done a lot of terminations, and it's really challenging to develop skills in letting an employee go when you haven't seen it done before. Additionally, at the core of many terminations is a sense that this is our fault or guilt that the fallout the employee will potentially experience is our fault. This guilt, although real, does not help grow your company. Instead it prevents top performance.

If you're a fast-driving manager at a big corporation, you have a human resources department and a lot of resources and training to help you through the process. But entrepreneurs often do not have any real management training, not to mention training in human resources.

So this book is really written for the entrepreneur. I want to help each of you grow your business by overcoming one of the hurdles that is preventing you from doing that—continuing to employ people who are no longer a good fit and are preventing the growth that you want. My system can help you learn to terminate people in a low-risk way and in a way that reduces the drama that can impact your company negatively as well.

Throughout the book, I refer to my own experiences and growth from learning from the difficult situations I have faced and mistakes I have made. I also reference my former boss, who my wife and I bought our current practice from. He started the firm from nothing and grew it into the 20-plus-employee establishment he sold to us. Over the course of his career, he remained self-employed, and he was very successful at it. But I watched him struggle with the termination process. He definitely struggled with letting people go, and he kept employees longer than he should have. In this book I've included examples of when, had he let the offending employee go earlier, he could have avoided a lot of dramatic and harmful situations that prevented his business from being as successful as possible.

I have also known other business owners and company leaders who have struggled to terminate employees. Perhaps it's an office manager that they've had for a long time, a friend that helped start the company, or even an employee that's just going through a really hard life experience or because the company is taking a different turn and the employee can no longer keep up with the role. Whatever the reason, I have seen numerous companies that are preventing the success of their own company by hanging onto poor-performing employees.

## CONTROLLING WHAT YOU CAN

Throughout my career, I've had to develop a system to help me effectively let people go. My system is based on coming up with a solution for every possible situation that I think I can control.

For example, I can't control the emotions that an employee is going to feel, but I can control my own emotions. I can't control what the employee will say when we're in the termination room, but I can write out what I want to say, and I can control what I say and how I say it. I can't control an employee wanting to make a scene, but I can control how and when I not only ask an employee to leave the premises but what precautions I have taken to prevent him from having access to anything sensitive after he's been told he's being let go. I can also control the aftermath of the termination, including how the company will move on and become a better-functioning firm and how my employees will respond to that.

In the following chapters, I outline my system. I start by taking a look at the long-term benefits of letting someone go and how keeping them onboard is potentially harming your company.

In my opinion, the hardest piece for any business owner to overcome when he's trying to decide to let someone go is his own emotional response, marked by fear, guilt, and hesitation. Controlling those emotions is the best way to help you get over that reaction and build your resolve to decide to go forward.

I'll also discuss that difficult point of actually deciding that you need to let an employee go. I'll share with you some exercises to help you take some comfort in knowing that this is the right decision, even though it's a very hard decision to execute.

I'll talk about how to prepare for the act of terminating someone, including preparing for both the bigger-picture items—like when the act will occur and who you're going to replace that person with—along with how you'll replace him or her and the specific circumstances surrounding the act of meeting with an employee and terminating him or her.

Other questions I'll answer include: Where will the act occur? How will you control your emotions? What security methods can you put in place to prevent dramatic scenes and legal risks?

I'll talk about the actual termination conversation itself. It's a very emotional and challenging conversation, and the only way to actually get better at it is to do it.

My system includes performing the act of terminating someone in a separate room. I'll also talk about how to control the events in that room, including how to let the employee release the emotions he's feeling in a controlled environment where it's very non-damaging to the rest of your staff. Remember: the responsibility of the employer to his employee after a termination is not so much to make sure that the terminated employee lands on his feet as quickly as possible or to help make sure his feelings aren't hurt but to be professional and appropriate throughout the situation to create a better sense of closure for the employee, too.

Finally, I'll also talk about what to do in the aftermath in terms of how you present this to the rest of your employees and how you move your company forward.

By reading this book and following the steps that I outline, you will move closer to your goal of solving the problems that are preventing you from having the company you desire.

# CHAPTER
# 1

## WE ALL STRUGGLE WITH DECIDING TO LET SOMEONE GO

Every business owner that I know who runs a successful business has had to terminate someone. That's me. I'm a successful business owner, and I've terminated a lot of people.

We've all been at a company where there is an employee who is either underperforming or has a negative attitude, and nobody is doing anything about it. We've seen how disruptive that is. As a business owner, it is our obligation to remove those people from the business.

However, every business owner that I've ever met has really struggled with having to go through with a termination. We all get better at it; it gets easier, but it never gets easy. We always carry some anxiety with every single decision—I've certainly carried my share of anxiety, and I still get butterflies, even though I've terminated people dozens of times.

One thing every business leader struggles with is how to know when it's the right time to let somebody go. But if you're determined to stay in business, sometimes you'll be forced to terminate an employee whose behavior or performance is detrimental to operations. If you've never done it, or have little experience at doing it, how do you do it properly and minimize your risks?

As a manager of 100 employees, I have been through this challenge a number of times. Even though, through trial and error, I've created a system that really works, the truth is that I'm still nervous every single time I have to let somebody go. I'm nervous when I make the decision, and I'm nervous when I get up from my chair and walk the hall to the conference room where the termination will occur. But the process of letting someone go does get easier over time as you get better at it.

I remember the first time that I ever let somebody go. She was an entry-level clerk, and she had only been with us six weeks. This is one of the least stressful terminations that any manager can ever do, letting someone go who is in a very entry-level position, has only been with the company for a very brief period of time, and has not developed any real roots or created any lasting relationships with other people. But I struggled with it all night. I didn't get very much sleep. It was a very challenging process to realize that I was going to do it for the first time and then to actually go through with it.

Over the course of several years and letting several people go, I've honed that process down in terms of what to say, how to say it, when to say it, and how to listen to somebody to allow them to let some of their emotions out. Through the evolution of this process, I've developed a system that allows me to have much less anxiety when the time comes to make the tough decision. Even though I'm still nervous during the act itself, that's a very brief period of anxiety compared to holding onto all those bad feelings for days leading up to the act.

## IN MY EXPERIENCE

When I was an associate attorney, an employee, I watched my boss, who was otherwise brilliant, really struggle with deciding to actually let somebody go. As a result of his inability to make a decision on the matter, he would repeatedly bring people into a conference room to reprimand them.

I particularly remember a regularly occurring incident that would happen when one employee—a manager—would turn in his report. Almost every week, my old boss would take the manager into a conference room and scream at him at the top of his lungs.

But when I would ask him, "Why don't you just fire this guy?" He would say, "I can't do that. He has a kid." And it was a different excuse every time. "I can't do that. He just got married. He has bills." He had all these excuses as to why he couldn't decide to actually terminate someone's employment.

This went on for about two years. What's worse was that the entire office would hear it. It was pretty upsetting for the other employees to witness, and it really stopped production. So the result was about two years of a dynamic that I think was probably horrible for the manager to live through but was even more detrimental to my boss and the firm as a whole. It seemed very hard on to the manager, it wasn't healthy for the office, and it wasn't healthy for my old boss.

That situation taught me that it's vital to make the decision that you need to let someone go for the health of the company.

While a similar situation may not exist in your organization, the reality is that we all struggle with coming to the determination that it is time to let someone go. But it is a necessary part of doing business if you're going to keep your company healthy.

Even if you've got some experience at terminating employees, chances are you struggle with the emotional side of the issue. Letting someone go can create just as much internal conflict for the person doing the firing as it does for the employee being let go.

This was definitely true for me early in my career, and I still struggle with it today.

I remember two specific instances where it was particularly gut-wrenching to let someone go. Even after a leader has been through the process a few times, there are just some instances that are more difficult than others to overcome. Here are a couple of examples where I really struggled even though I had already been through the process of terminating employees.

## Case 1
## Letting a Friend Go

The first example of a difficult termination occurred when I was an owner of the firm. We hired an attorney who I almost instantly became friends with. We were a similar age, we were both interested in the same hobbies, and we were both into sports, and so we ended up hanging out socially outside of work. In addition, our wives got along. So all in all, we developed a pretty good friendship.

But after two years of working together, Karen and I began to realize that this attorney I viewed as my friend actually wasn't very good at his job. He wasn't a great fit as an employee in the firm, even though he and I were really good friends. He was a great guy to go have a beer with, but when it came to work-related issues, he either didn't have a good answer for the problem or situation at hand, or it was very challenging to deal with him about any particular matter. In fact, he had a bit of a defiant personality.

Seeing this, I started to entertain the idea that he was not a good fit to have at the firm. But it took almost a year to actually acknowledge and decide that we needed to go through with the termination because the dynamics just made the decision so difficult. After all, he was a friend, I had been to his house, he knew my kids, and we had that personal relationship.

I think many business owners struggle with having an employee that they've grown too close with personally who's actually not a great fit work-wise.

Looking back, I realize it took way too long to decide to let him go. Once the decision was made, and he was let go, the friendship was over. Ultimately, I realized that the truth is that I offered a good job with a good salary, and he didn't appreciate it. The friendship was over, but a true friend wants your company to do well and wants to do great work for you.

I think this is true for a lot of business owners. They're too close to an employee, and the reality is that employee is taking advantage of them, and they're not actually being a good friend.

## Case 2
## The Strong Personality

Another example of when the decision was really hard for me was when the firm had another manager who had a very strong personality. She really dominated her team, so her team never complained about her. My partner and I would hear rumors that it was difficult for other managers and other leaders in the firm to work with her, but it felt like her work was getting done, and her team never complained. It was hard for us to identify that she was actually a problem.

Ultimately, we found evidence that she was stealing from us. Even then, when we started asking questions about what we discovered, it was very challenging to find anybody who was willing to say that they worked directly with her and that she was a problem. She basically had this intimidating presence.

When we decided to go through with the act of letting her go, it was a very tense situation in the conference room, which I'll talk about how to deal with in later chapters.

But again, this example was a matter of dealing with a personality that was very intimidating and very strong-willed, so it made the entire process a real struggle. It was a real struggle to decide letting her go was the right thing to do, a real struggle to corroborate that decision with actual evidence from others, and a real struggle to go through with the actual act of letting her go.

## A BOTTOM-LINE DECISION

Once a manager gets the termination process down, he can focus more on the business operation and on keeping the company moving forward.

In my experience, from the time you start to struggle with an employee until the time they are out the door, a portion of your attention during every waking minute is spent distracted by that disruptive employee, by the act of letting that employee go, by the act of questioning your decision, and by the emotions that you have. Every single ounce of your attention is divided, at all times, with this problem just kind of lingering out there.

But the sooner you can get the termination process down—you're able to decide more quickly that it's time to let somebody go, and you're able to go through with the process—you relieve yourself of that distraction, and you're able to keep the company going forward. Until then, anytime you have to let someone go, you're going to be operating at half strength until you make that decision and you go through with that process.

## PREVENTATIVE MEASURES

I'm not a human resources attorney—I'm a businessman. So while I have tried-and-true practices for letting people go, it's still a good idea to check with your internal human resources professionals or an outside human resources attorney for legal advice. This is a message I'll repeat throughout the book.

That said, there are two golden rules for protecting yourself from legal action when it comes to letting people go: one is to hire well, and the other is to fire well.

Let's look at the first of these: hiring well.

The best defense against letting people go is to hire well. And the key to hiring well is to understand yourself as a business owner. This is different than understanding yourself as a person. As a man or a woman you might think, "I'm into fitness," or "I'm into football," or "I'm into drinking beer," or "I'm into church." All of those are social activities, and that's how we relate to people on a personal level.

Most business owners that I know, including myself, have a different personality at work than we do socially. We're a different person. Sometimes friends or family come visit me at the office and I feel almost awkward, like this isn't the right place for me to talk to them because I'm in my business mode.

So again, the first piece to hiring well is to understand yourself as a business owner. This can be a real challenge, because the truth is, most business owners who run a successful company are terrible at evaluating themselves.

---

## THREE KEYS TO HIRING WELL

Hire employees with similar passion.

Use third-party testing to determine if a person will be a good fit.

Know what to look for in the resume.

---

### 1. Hire employees with similar passion

Start by asking yourself some questions: What's your passion? What's your personality? What makes you tick? What are your career goals? Then, when you hire, find people who have similar goals and ambitions. You want people who can match your passion. Maybe you like to just sit on the couch on Sundays and watch football, not doing any exercise at all, but then when you go into work on Monday you hit the ground running—you walk fast and are really intense about getting certain deadlines met. Those two personas are vastly different.

It's the same at work in terms of hiring. Find that individual that has the ambitions and passion to meet the goals you set for your company.

What I've found while managing over 100 employees is that the people who stimulate you back are the ones who are the easiest to work with and the ones who are easiest to solve problems with. They're the ones who operate with passion similar to yours.

What really helps me understand who I'm looking for in an employee is to consider who else in the company I enjoy exchanging ideas with. What makes that person tick? What makes that dynamic work well? If I could select somebody to work with on a project, who would I choose? Once I identify that person or those people, then I ask myself what those people are like. What makes them enjoyable to work with? Is it because they are able to listen to all of my proposals and recognize the ones that are really good and then run with those? Do they have some intuition on why the other proposals are bad? Do they actually come back to me with their own ideas?

Sometimes business owners prefer to work with people who just "get them" but don't bring a lot of ideas to the table; they don't want a lot of discussion, they just want the job done. Other business owners really value a back-and-forth exchange. And then there are business owners who are charismatic, energized personalities, and they like people who they can really get fired up and together they get things going.

## 2. Use third-party testing to determine if a person will be a good fit

The second piece to hiring well, I've found, is to use online surveys that grade a person's aptitude in terms of their ability to handle certain stress levels, be clear on certain decisions, and be strong on certain tasks. To pay a little bit of money for one of those surveys and to have potential new hires take one can go a long way towards more frequently hiring good people.

## 3. Know what to look for in the resume

The third piece to hiring well is to really look at the resume. The one piece of evidence I've found to be helpful in a person's resume—beyond the degrees and job experience—is the person's tenure in previous jobs. In my experience, it doesn't matter whether a candidate went to a great school or has a 4.0 grade point average. Even if she went to a community college or had really low test scores, she can still be a great employee.

What I've found to be the best indicator of poor performance is when someone has jumped from job to job. That usually means there's a string of employers who either terminated that person or knew enough about the person to make him not feel welcome.

I've found that, during the interview, having a second person that you trust in the room is invaluable. Again, the key is to trust them. I've had people in the room with me that weren't necessarily my favorite people to work with, but I felt they had a good enough understanding of me and of the needs of the position and the company, and I trusted them enough to have them in the interview room.

If you don't have the luxury of having a second person in the room during the initial process, then it's imperative to have at least a second interview before hiring someone.

So hiring well has brought me my greatest successes and least amount of grief over having to let someone go.

When it comes to firing well, the best success will come from having a system in place for doing so.

This begins with having a standard in place for measuring performance. I've developed two different systems for doing this.

The first is having a simple graph or data reports that show how much an individual employee is actually producing at his job post. See Examples A and B below and in the Appendix. With this method, the only real way to understand if the data is beneficial is to have a second person perform the same or similar job function. This starts to let you have a measure of the reasonable amount of production you can expect for that job post.

## SANDWICH PRODUCTION
### PER HOUR

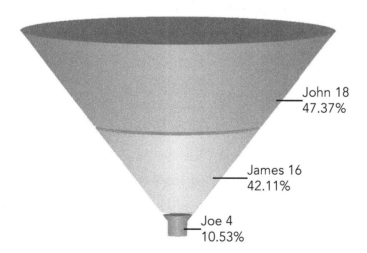

John 18
47.37%

James 16
42.11%

Joe 4
10.53%

Example A

| SANDWICH | TIME | USER |
|:---:|:---:|:---:|
| Tuna | 12:02 | James |
| BLT | 12:09 | James |
| BLT | 12:10 | James |
| BLT | 12:13 | James |
| Ham | 12:15 | James |
| Tuna | 12:20 | James |
| PB&J | 12:24 | James |
| PB&J | 12:25 | James |
| Tuna | 12:27 | James |
| Ham | 12:31 | James |
| Tuna | 12:33 | James |
| BLT | 12:35 | James |
| Ham | 12:37 | James |
| Ham | 12:41 | James |
| Tuna | 12:44 | James |
| BLT | 12:51 | James |
| Ham | 12:02 | Joe |
| BLT | 12:17 | Joe |

Example B

The second piece is a performance evaluation log. This charts out all the expectations that you have for an employee—what you don't want an employee to do and what you do want him to do—which is produce. See Example C below and in the Appendix. The performance log at our firm shows that we don't value employees who don't produce work, make a lot of mistakes, or have a disruptive attitude.

# Employee Evaluation Log

Name of Employee    *Jim*

| Date/Day | Number of Violations | Number of Sandwiches Produced | Comments |
|---|---|---|---|
| Monday | 3 | 13 | late for work |
| Tuesday | 2 | 18 | |
| Wednesday | 0 | 14 | |
| Thursday | 0 | 19 | |
| Friday | 1 | 17 | late for work |

# Comparison Analysis

Name of Employee    *Jim*

| Ideal Qualities For Position | Actual Abilities |
|---|---|
| Hard working, always on time, positive attitude | Struggles to be on time. Sometimes has a negative attitude. |
| Skilled at making sandwiches with a smile and greeting customers | Not as friendly as I would like. |
| Produces at least 25 sandwiches per hour of employment | Has never produced 25 sandwiches in an hour. |
| Eager to take on new tasks when store is slow | I have to constantly ask if Jim is available for other tasks. |

Example C

If an employee does any of the aforementioned—he doesn't produce, makes a lot of mistakes, or has a very disruptive attitude—then we have protocols for either changing that behavior or for beginning the termination process. I developed and follow a four-step process, which will be discussed in more detail in chapter 3. The four steps are: verbal warning; written warning; second written warning with an intensely candid (and almost harsh) in-person meeting about your concerns; and termination.

With this standard in place for measuring performance—a matrix or reports along with an evaluation log—it's much easier to know when the time is right to let someone go. This standard helps you be consistent and better protected legally, and it allows you to be more transparent with your employees—they know what to expect from you.

The performance evaluation log also allows us to see which employees are attempting to get back in the good graces with the firm.

---

## THREE KEYS FOR FIRING WELL

Use a simple matrix or reports to show how much an individual employee is actually producing at his job post.

Use a performance evaluation log to write out all the expectations that you have for an employee.

Have protocols in place that start with a verbal warning for a first offense, followed by a written warning for a second offense, and then a second written warning for a third offense. With the next offense, the employment is terminated.

---

In my company, if an employee doesn't produce very well and receives a verbal warning and then still doesn't produce very well, he gets a written warning. But then if he has a month or a couple of months in a row where he starts to improve—he starts to produce more—then we start to give him good evaluations. These also go in the employee's file, and that brings him down a notch from the written-warning level to the verbal-warning level. It lowers his status and moves him farther away from a possible termination.

Having a system like this protects the business owner. It gives you a way to confront employees that are not doing well and lets you talk to them about how they can do better. Then if they actually start to improve their performance, it serves as a system for getting them back on the right path so they don't remain on the verge of almost losing their job.

## HOW TO FEEL BETTER AFTERWARD

Although this will be covered in more detail in a later chapter, it's important to have a brief discussion here about feeling better after the termination.

What I have found is that, when the actual termination is done, I instantly feel better. It's a really big relief. I've had a lot of anxiety going into the process and getting through the act itself, and now that the act is done, I instantly feel better.

This is a good thing, but feeling better after the act is an emotional response, and it doesn't solve the entire problem surrounding the act of letting someone go.

The bigger problem is: How do we keep our company moving forward?

The key to truly experiencing a better feeling is to have a plan in place so that a couple of weeks, a month, or two months later, you look back and say, "That was a great decision. The company is better off now."

As early as possible, when you're entertaining that struggle of whether you should let someone go, you should start to ask yourself questions about what you need to do to replace that person if you do let him go. What is your plan to move forward with the position? Implementing that strategy to cover the workload and the position and evaluating how long it will take to get someone else in the position and up to speed are the best ways of making yourself feel better after the fact. That's what improves your company, which is what you're always trying to do.

## IT'S ABOUT THE BUSINESS

Ultimately, if you're a responsible business owner, being about the business first is bigger than just being about your own process. It's about the key people who you're employing and their livelihoods, and the entry-level people you're employing may not rely on this position for a mortgage or a family, but they may rely on it to be a first stepping-stone toward a better career.

If you have an employee who is underperforming or disruptive and you're asking yourself those tough questions about letting him go, you have to remember it's not just about you, the business leader, or the company's profits, nor is it just about the employee and his job. It's about putting the entire business ahead of that underperforming employee. It's about all those other jobs and all the other people whose production or morale is being hampered. It's about those people not getting full satisfaction out of the job that you're offering them. It's about the rest of the people who work for you being able to better themselves, get ahead in life, maybe advance their resume, and grow as a person.

In my experience, every employee has some awareness about every other employee. If you're the business owner and you're beginning to notice that an employee is either underperforming or he has a bad attitude, and you're starting to ask yourself if he should go, then other employees are also asking themselves the same question. If this goes on too long, good employees start to wonder if negative behavior is tolerated.

If you don't take action to address the problem, then you're sending the wrong message to the rest of your team—the good employees who are doing their jobs. You're sending the message that negative behavior is tolerated. Employees may begin to feel there is favoritism occurring, or in the worst case, there could be pretty severe consequences such as claims of workplace harassment or other legal allegations against you as the business owner.

Probably, more commonly, good employees won't want to work in an environment that tolerates bad employee behavior and they'll end up quitting.

Deciding to let someone go and then actually going through with the act is a serious obligation for any business owner who wants to be respected by good employees and wants to run a business that's successful. It sends the right message that you won't tolerate bad behavior, and it helps keep up the morale of the rest of the good employees.

It's not a choice. The only choice you have in a situation like this is whether to investigate when you believe there's a problem. Once you have the data or the information to make a decision, it's no longer a choice. It's an obligation. The other option is to have a very poorly run company that either goes out of business or that struggles to maintain any kind of profit.

# Chapter 1 Takeaways

1} A graph (Example A)

**SANDWICH PRODUCTION**
PER HOUR

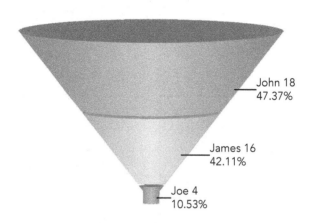

John 18
47.37%

James 16
42.11%

Joe 4
10.53%

2} Data report (Example B)

| SANDWICH | TIME | USER |
|----------|------|------|
| Tuna | 12:02 | James |
| BLT | 12:09 | James |
| BLT | 12:10 | James |
| BLT | 12:13 | James |
| Ham | 12:15 | James |
| Tuna | 12:20 | James |
| PB&J | 12:24 | James |
| PB&J | 12:25 | James |
| Tuna | 12:27 | James |
| Ham | 12:31 | James |
| Tuna | 12:33 | James |

| BLT | 12:35 | James |
|-----|-------|-------|
| Ham | 12:37 | James |
| Ham | 12:41 | James |
| Tuna | 12:44 | James |
| BLT | 12:51 | James |
| Ham | 12:02 | Joe |
| BLT | 12:17 | Joe |

## 3} A sample performance evaluation log (Example C)

| Date/Day | Number of Violations | Number of Sandwiches Produced | Comments |
|----------|---------------------|------------------------------|----------|
| Monday | 3 | 13 | late for work |
| Tuesday | 2 | 18 | |
| Wednesday | 0 | 14 | |
| Thursday | 0 | 19 | |
| Friday | 1 | 17 | late for work |

| Ideal Qualities For POsition | Actual Abilities |
|------------------------------|------------------|
| Hard working, always on time, positive attitude | Struggles to be on time. Sometimes has a negative attitude. |
| Skilled at making sandwiches with a smile and greeting customers | Not as friendly as I would like. |
| Produces at least 25 sandwiches per hour of employment | Has never produced 25 sandwiches in an hour. |
| Eager to take on new tasks when store is slow | I have to constantly ask if Jim is available for other tasks. |

4} 3 Tips for Hiring Well:

Understand yourself as a business owner, then hire individuals whose personalities match your own.

Use online surveys that grade a person's aptitude.

Scrutinize the resume; consider a person's tenure with past jobs.

5} 3 Tips for Firing Well:

Use a simple graph or reports to show how much an individual employee is actually producing at his job post.

Use a performance evaluation log to write out all the expectations that you have for an employee.

Have protocols in place that start with a verbal warning for a first offense, followed by a written warning for a second offense, and then a second written warning for a third offense. With the next offense, the employment is terminated.

# CHAPTER
# 2

## SEEING THE SIGNS, MAKING THE DECISION

When you decide to terminate an employee, ultimately you want your decision to be as rational as possible. You want it to be void of any emotions. Your decision should be based on facts that are as accurate and as complete as possible.

So what do you do when operations are moving along just fine and then something changes in an employee's attitude? The first step is to recognize that something is amiss. Often, it's one of several scenarios.

### Scenario 1
### Struggling New Hire

I encourage giving a new hire a certain period of time to catch onto the duties of his job. Make sure you are consistent with how much time you allow. If after this period of time he just doesn't seem to understand the role, despite your training efforts, he should go. To me, this is the easiest and most obvious situation in which you can catch the problem early and decide quickly that the employee needs to be let go.

Usually, this happens in one of two ways.

One way is that the new hire comes in and is given tasks to perform, but he just can't seem to catch on. The expected outcomes for these tasks are based on the performance of other employees in the same or similar positions. The key to identifying a problem quickly with the new hire is to continuously collect data on what each role in your company is able to produce, and then retain those stats. Then, when you have a new hire, you have data to compare against that role's performance. This allows you to have certain expectations that should begin day one and then be measurable after week one, week two, month one, the six-week mark, and then in two-week increments. You should have set standards of where the employee should be at those points and all the way through a 90-day trial period.

At any point, if the employee is not hitting his marks, you need to act quickly before you invest valuable training resources. The people in your company who are training these new hires are likely very good at their own jobs, and if they were not involved in training, they could give you more production. So it's important to eliminate poor-performing new hires as quickly as possible.

The second way in which an employee fails to catch on in a timely manner is a little bit trickier to deal with. This is when you've had an employee who is with you for a little while longer and then he moves into a new role and doesn't catch on to the task at the new role as quickly as you would like. Maybe the person was successful at the previous job, and he had good energy in that role. He was up for a challenge and you had a need, so you moved him into a new position. Unfortunately, he's just not catching on.

This example is more challenging, because if he is moving into a new role then two things are probably true. One, he's been with you for a while, so he probably knows how your business operates, which has some value. And two, for some reason, you've chosen him to move, and so you thought it was going to work.

In this second example, follow the same protocol as in the first example, which is to have established criteria for where the employee should be in his new role after his first day, first week, second week, first month, six weeks, and so on through 90 days.

However, depending on the person in this situation, you may want to build in the option to move the employee back to his old position rather than actually let him go. With this example, it's a little more challenging to actually make the decision to let this person go because he may have done a good job in another area of the company before he moved into a new position.

In this example, it's critical to ensure that the employee is given every opportunity to catch on to the new job. Part of that involves making sure that the person training the employee in his new role really understands that role himself and is also a good trainer. If the training itself is at fault for the employee not learning the new role, then you'll get misleading results indicating that the employee doesn't have the aptitude to do the job, when in reality he does; he's just paired with an ineffective teacher.

Having a good trainer is vital to getting accurate information to determine whether an advancing employee has the ability to do the job.

# Scenario 2
## Eroding Attitude

A scenario that needs to be closely watched by leadership is that of a person who has been with the company for a long time and then is turned down for advancement. He has asked for a promotion, a different position, or additional responsibility, but for whatever reason, he's turned down. You just don't think he's right for the position he requested.

In my experience, the person who asks for something and doesn't get it needs to be watched very closely because his attitude can quickly erode.

For example, we had a receptionist who was very pleasant and very good at greeting people. She was congenial and had a nice smile, but beyond greeting people, the work she did for the company was barely mediocre, at best.

She would pretty regularly ask for more responsibility but was repeatedly turned down because again, beyond greeting people, she really wasn't getting her work done.

This escalated very quickly into her becoming a poor employee, and we ended up having to let her go as a result. We made the decision to terminate her employment based on the way she handled the news that we weren't going to move her to a different role.

Unfortunately, some employees are a contradiction between what they say they want and how they perform. On the one hand they can't handle—and they even resist—the tasks that are assigned to them, but on the other hand they are quick to ask for a promotion and more responsibility.

It is very tempting for any business owner who is beaten down with burdens, responsibilities, and stresses all day to give more responsibility to someone who essentially raises his hand and asks for it. But don't be fooled by the person who does this when he is not even good at the job he has, because chances are very good that he will not pick up other tasks either. Sometimes his actions are a ploy to maneuver around within the company and hide from actually being tasked with the responsibility of getting just one job done. Sometimes it's just a matter of the person not having a realistic view of himself.

Whatever the case, this is not someone who should be moved quickly. And when you deny him advancement, you'll continue to see his self-view is unrealistic. Rather than admit he's not ready for a move or that your reasons are justified, he'll continue to believe he is deserving, and his attitude will erode.

He ends up causing a situation that can only end one way—which is with you making the decision to let them go.

## Scenario 3
## Sinking Celebrated Employee

A particularly challenging scenario is the one in which an employee, who at some point was a celebrated performer, but now is no longer up to par. He's received good reviews, maybe raises, and possibly promotions, but something happened along the way, and now he's no longer a productive employee.

It's very challenging to make the decision to let this person go because the first thing that you tend to do as a business owner is remember his past highlights.

For example, an attorney who worked for us did a great job. He got everything done that we asked him to do, and we gave him raises over time. Then something happened in his personal life that caused him to just stop caring about the job. He eventually hit a point where he just could not produce, and we had to move on as a business. It was a very difficult decision because he had given us a lot over time. But as a business owner, you always have to be forward thinking, and you have to think about the greater good of the company. So we had to make the decision to end his employment.

In another instance, we had an employee who was very good at what he did, but he was a very introverted person. He never really spoke up and never asserted any of his concerns, and then one day, suddenly, he turned in his notice. When we asked him why he wanted to leave, he just replied that he was burned out with the tasks he was doing. Looking back, we saw that his production had been declining in the months before his departure. We would have been better served to realize that quicker and make the decision ourselves to let him go.

It is quite possible that a good employee will experience burn out from the tasks he's been given and will never say anything, and his performance will dip to the point where you are best served just to let him go.

## Scenario 4
## The Drama King/Queen

Some people are quick to feel anxiety, which causes them to have a frantic but high-paced energy. This person presents a "fake out" where he appears to look busy all the time, but he's really not producing the results you are looking for.

Typically, you give him some tasks and he performs them pretty well. He looks super busy, and he walks around the office with a lot of passion. But he always has a stressed look, and if you are a busy business owner, you may not be paying attention to notice that he is actually not getting much done.

Regardless of past praise that was based on a misinterpretation of the frantic energy, he's actually not producing very much, and he needs to be let go as quickly as possible—his frantic, tense attitude is actually causing harm in his immediate work environment.

We had an employee who was with our firm for six years, and for the first five and a half years, I thought he was one of our best employees. Anything that I personally asked him to get done, he would get done. And he would get it done with a lot of quality.

He always seemed to walk with seriousness and purpose. He always seemed to be busy at his desk.

But over the years, I heard comments from others about how he would yell swear words, and slam things at his desk, or he would mutter negative comments about how he couldn't handle the work. I always dismissed those rumors because I thought he was working hard, and I thought he really cared about the job. It wasn't until I had been working with him for five and a half years that I developed a matrix to look at his work production.

That's when I realized he actually wasn't getting much work done at all. When I, as the business owner, asked him to do something, he would go and get that done. But otherwise, he basically just sat at his desk with a really intense personality and burned a lot of calories that didn't provide any results.

So not only did we decide it was best to let him go, but we found out that he was actually causing a lot of stress and strain to his coworkers who sat around him and witnessed this frantic, stressful behavior.

In the end, it was a sort of a double win to get someone who could produce better and have a calmer demeanor, resulting in a calmer environment.

## Scenario 5
## One Employee for the Price of Two

Another case of missing the mark with an employee is when you have someone who has been with the company for a while, and now he's overpaid. Over time, you've given him good reviews and raises, but somewhere along the line you miscalculated his pay and the next thing you know he's earning double what the starting pay for that position would be. Yet he's not producing what two people would be producing.

For example, we employed an attorney for several years and he did do a good job, he got work done, and we gave him a raise every year because we felt compelled to do so. Then, after years of raises, we realized he was still doing a good job but wasn't doing enough work to equal the production of two employees, even though his salary was what we would be paying two employees in this position.

This can be a really challenging situation. Often, the right move is not to let the person go but to find some other solution.

In this situation, you need to have a conversation with the employee to explain the situation to him fully and to tell him that you may need to assign him different or additional responsibilities, or you may need to ask them to take a pay cut. Usually having a conversation in this situation is better than deciding to let the person go.

Make sure in this scenario that the decisions you're making are within legal boundaries. For example, if you're dealing with an employee who has been with you for decades, you may be in a position where you have given him too many raises and his pay has exceeded his ability to adequately produce. This can lead to a lot of problems, including issues with the employee's age.

The best way to deal with the problem of having an employee who is overpaid is to avoid the situation altogether by having a good system for giving pay raises and reviews. If you have an employee who's producing excellent work, then it's easy to give him good raises, and if you have an employee who's performing poorly, then he won't receive any raises. In fact, it may be easier to let him go. The midlevel employee who may never be a star performer but who will remain with your company for many years can be hard to evaluate. If you give a raise every year, you will likely find yourself overpaying for the production you are getting.

The key preventive measure is to have a good system in place to give appropriate reviews and pay raises that aren't too elaborate and don't reward mediocre performance beyond what's appropriate.

## Scenario 6
## The Negative Attitude

Sometimes the problem is a personality conflict between the business owner and the employee who is otherwise a pretty good employee. This is a person who produces results on his stat sheet but also has a pretty bad attitude.

Usually he's not just crusty to deal with, but he actually seems to be resentful to the business owners themselves.

We had an employee who was with the firm for a long time. We gave him raises and a lot of responsibility—we even trusted him to run the office when we were out on vacation or out of the office for a work trip.

After about four years, we started to hear reports that while we were gone, he was telling other people that he was angry that we weren't in the office enough. He even made a comment to one person that if we wanted something done, we needed to come back from vacation and get it done ourselves. He grew to be very divisive when we were not in the office—for example, going through the payroll and scoffing at certain salaries.

When we found out about his antics, making the decision to let him go was a challenge because he was such a high producer—he was very good at his job and was getting the work done that needed to be done.

Even if an employee is producing results with a bad attitude, he needs to be removed from your company. You need to make the decision to terminate his employment because he is too disruptive for those employees who are loyal to you and who are also producing. Those employees need to see that you won't tolerate this person's behavior, and they deserve a better environment than you're allowing by keeping this person in your office.

One of the problems with this tyrannical, negative personality is that he can end up holding good workers hostage. Most people are conditioned to have an attitude of, "Oh, I don't want to get anyone in trouble. Therefore, I'll never say anything," or, "I don't want to be the one to get involved with that. I'll just do my job."

Even if the good workers' emotions aren't being brought down severely enough that they themselves are not doing enough work, these more levelheaded employees would oftentimes rather just look for another job than tell the boss about a problem employee.

Sometimes, it's nearly impossible for the boss or the business owner to get firsthand accounts of the tyrannical employee, because many people can be intimidated by such a personality in the workplace. Many people aren't accustomed to working with a really strong, loud personality, so they don't say anything.

As a business owner, when you hear those whispers or allegations that someone is making a scene, damaging your property, or disrupting coworkers, you need to take it very seriously. You need to do as thorough an investigation as possible.

Sit down with the employees privately and assure them you just want information and you won't reveal their name. Ask them the same or similar questions three or four times because employees are so averse to "tattling" on their coworkers, especially if their coworker is an intimidating, loud personality.

In the end, unless you have the emotional bandwidth and resources to properly coach and manage an employee who is otherwise ineffective—maybe his personality isn't a match, or he's not fast enough, or he's too fast, or he's too emotional—he isn't going to be a good fit in your organization, and you need to part ways.

## RECOGNIZING THE PROBLEM, MAKING THE DECISION

Once you get an inkling that there's a problem in your company, sometimes it can take a while before you can wrap your mind around what to do.

The first step is recognizing that you have a problem and coming to the decision that you need to act on it.

There are two tricks that have helped me get to the next step of the process.

The first is to try to picture the company with somebody else handling the position that the current troublesome employee holds. I try to do this in a way where I completely black out the uncomfortable situation of actually letting the person go. I black out all of the painful parts of going through that process.

Instead, I try to envision the company in the future. I picture it six months from now with a different person in that role. I meditate on that picture and let the idea marinate while I decide whether that company of the future seems to be in a better place. That image of a different company without the potentially problem employee and removing the obsession over the act of going through the termination can give me a really helpful picture in a non-stressful way.

That picture also helps support that the decision to let the employee go is the right one to make.

If I can't act on a decision right away or I just can't make a decision, then the second trick I use is to send myself a meeting appointment anywhere from one week to three weeks out to prompt me to revisit the problem. This trick allows me, for the time being, to free my mind of the issue and focus on other, more immediate tasks, instead of holding onto it because it's an unfinished problem.

# DEALING WITH INDECISION

Sometimes you recognize that there is a problem with an employee, but you still have to deal with the voice in your head that says maybe this situation is different.

For example, I remember one attorney who worked for us, and when I first started to entertain the idea that he should be let go, I didn't want it to be true. I considered him a friend. I thought of times when we had hung out together outside of work, and I also knew he was a very strong personality, and it would be challenging to go through with the act.

The first thing I felt was a very strong negative emotion—again, that I didn't want it to be true. But when I started to consider the situation further, I began to conclude that letting him go might be the right decision.

Often, after that first negative reaction, you start to see the upside of the situation. You start to see the employee in a positive light. You start to believe that the employee is doing a really good job on a project—he's saying the right things in meetings, or he's supporting a new initiative. In other words, he's doing something that makes him look more attractive than you had been giving him credit for.

This can be a very challenging situation, but it's also a ruse. Usually, the person is the same at all times, and it's our own inner guilt and fear of going through with the act that's causing us to be the devil's advocate to ourselves in this situation. Still, there's ultimately a reason why it's hard to come to a decision, probably because he's been with you for a while, and he's done a lot of positive things during that time. But in the end, he's just not doing enough.

Usually, your internal struggle is driven by the fear of having to go through with the act of terminating someone combined with concern about what will happen to the employee once he has lost his position. But once you are done with the act, you almost always realize it was the right decision and the right thing for the former employee too.

Your indecision over not wanting to let someone go is an emotional reaction. Dealing with this indecision is about being rational. Remember: if the employee was a really solid member of the team, then you wouldn't rationally entertain letting him go. The rational decision to let somebody go is almost always more accurate than the emotional pull of not wanting to let someone go. So it's important to let that rational voice work itself through.

One of the tricks to making the decision that I think is tremendously helpful is the exercise of writing out the problem and what you really want.

---

## TRY THIS EXERCISE

At the top of a piece of paper, write the job title or role of the person you are considering letting go, but don't put the person's name—for example, write the titles of attorney, accountant, clerk, receptionist, etc.

Next, write all of the tasks that you want that role to perform.

After that, write down what you would be willing to pay for those tasks to get done.

And finally, write down the attitude that you want the person in that role to have while he performs those tasks.

After you have listed these items, then write the employee's name on the paper, and going down the list, with each task, ask yourself: can he get this task done?

I have found that the answer is almost always obvious when I am studying the facts on a piece of paper.

This exercise allows you to look at the problem from a rational perspective. It allows you to examine the needs of the role or the job first before applying a name. When you distance yourself from the emotional piece of the situation, the reality becomes more obvious.

---

The problem with thinking about the issue emotionally is that we're relying on our opinions. We rationalize that the employee did a good job on one specific task while dismissing the last three weeks' worth of evidence proving the contrary.

To keep from basing your decision solely on opinion, write the problem out and be thorough about your data. With this method, the answer will become obvious to you.

Again, there are always risks when you are going to let someone go, so it's best to consult an outside human resources attorney—or your own human resources department if you have one—and to have a second, trusted opinion from within your own organization.

## EXCEPTIONS TO THE RULE

There are some exceptions to deciding to let somebody go. I touched on one earlier in the chapter—the example of the employee getting paid twice what the position is designed to pay, and even though he produces good work, he isn't producing enough to create value in his current position.

In that situation, it's better to have a conversation with the employee to explain that you're going to require more of him to better match the salary, or you may need to ask him to take a pay cut. Again, this is a situation where a conversation about changing expectations may be better than letting the person go.

Another exception is when, as a business owner, you feel betrayed by the employee for some reason and your emotions get the better of you.

One example that occurred in my organization was when a woman who started in an entry-level job was soon moved to another department because she appeared to have advanced skills better suited to a different position. My firm paid for her to get more training, and I mentored her over time. But then I found out that she was upset with me for not including her in some decisions and that she was looking for another job outside the firm.

My initial, emotional reaction was a sense of betrayal, followed by the decision to let her go. Since she had been a valuable employee, and the organization had invested resources in advancing her, I felt that she was not being loyal to the opportunities that we provided for her, and she wasn't really somebody I wanted to work at the firm.

But before I acted, I first consulted other people in the firm who reached out to her and found out that, in reality, she wanted to stay with the firm and work harder. She wanted more responsibility. I met with her, and we talked the situation over, and she ended up deciding to stay.

Today, she remains a very valuable—and loyal—employee.

In this situation, simply talking to the person face-to-face and airing out any grievances can make both parties feel better. Once there's a meeting of the minds, then the employee can get back to work and you end up with a better employee in the long term.

Finally, there's the situation where an employee takes a leave of absence for a time to deal with a personal issue, such as a divorce or the death of a family member. In situations like this, I mark a time six months out—after that person's return to his post—to gauge whether he's returned to his former level of productivity. Usually, I find, key employees are able to ramp back up to their former selves. If not, then after the six-month mark, it may be time to make a decision about meeting with or keeping that employee.

## AN OPEN-DOOR CULTURE

It's vital when you are trying to make solid decisions—and difficult decisions—about your personnel to have a culture that allows people to express their concerns about other employees.

If your business is large enough to support a human resources department, then it's a great move to have a human resources professional on staff that employees can feel safe to go to. This promotes an open-door environment that allows employees to express concerns about coworkers, which ultimately lets you, the business owner, know about certain personnel you may need to deal with.

If your business is not large enough to justify having a human resources department, then it's good to have a diverse group of key personnel that employees feel they can go to. This gives them a chance to choose who they feel most comfortable talking to when they have a concern.

For example, not everybody we employ is comfortable coming to me. But my partner, my wife, is often more approachable. Then again, sometimes both of us are too daunting, so we have an office manager who is a little younger than either of us, and she is sometimes more approachable when employees have a concern.

By having a way for employees to report when something is amiss, you are able to get valuable information to make good, rational decisions about who to let go.

The bottom line is that some employees are detrimental to your company, and you, as the business owner, need to decide what to do about the situation and be ready to take action. If you don't, you are the one harming your company.

Every business owner that has a profitable and sustainable company values his ability to make decisions. That's what sets us apart as business owners—making the big decisions in the face of risk. And what keeps your company healthy and vibrant is being able to make the decision to terminate an employee when the relationship is eroding. It's also what sets us apart as successful business owners— it's up to us to be the one person in the room who is able to rise above the emotions and make that key decision.

# Chapter 2 Takeaways

1} Don't know whether to let someone go? Try this exercise:

At the top of a piece of paper, write the job title or role of the person you are considering letting go, but don't put the person's name—for example, write attorney, accountant, clerk, receptionist, etc.

Next, write all of the tasks that you want that role to perform.

After that, write down what you would be willing to pay for those tasks to get done.

Finally, write down the attitude that you want that person to have while he performs those tasks.

After you list these items, then write the current employee's name on the paper, and go down the list and, with each task, ask yourself: Can he get this task done? What you'll find is that the answer is almost always no.

This exercise allows you to look at the problem from a rational perspective. It allows you to examine the needs of the role or the job first before applying a name. When you distance yourself from the emotional piece of the situation, the reality becomes more obvious.

2} Six Warning Signs That Something is Amiss With an Employee

Employee Struggling in a New Role: sometimes a new hire just can't seem to understand the duties of his job. Sometimes a person advances beyond his capabilities. In either of these instances, the best way to gauge performance is to have measurable expectations.

Eroding Attitude: when a longtime employee is denied advancement, his attitude may quickly erode.

Sinking Celebrated Employee: an employee who has been a longtime, celebrated performer may finally peak and then burn out and no longer be up to par.

The Drama King/Queen: an employee has a particularly harried personality, which can easily be mistaken as passion for the job.

Twice the Price Employee: without a good system in place for delivering pay raises, some employees may be given raises year after year without added responsibilities, until they are ultimately earning twice the salary their position typically pays.

The Negative Attitude: this is the employee that, overall, does a good job for the company but who seemingly resents management.

# CHAPTER
# 3

## SETTING IT UP

A s the business owner, it's critical that you remember that it's your business that's being affected and that the situation really needs to be resolved in a way that works best for you. If the company goes under, then the employees just go get other jobs, but you are the one stuck holding the bag.

It's important to time the act of terminating an employee so that, within reason, it benefits you, the business owner, and if possible, also the employee. But primarily, it should benefit you—you want to set up the timing in a way that works best for you, causes the least amount of disruption and risk possible.

First, let's look at a few situations that may delay the act of letting someone go.

# Situation 1
## Keeping the Employee On to Finish a Project

The first situation is the challenge of keeping someone on a little while longer to finish a project, even after you know there's a problem and have decided to let him go.

This happened with me when we were expanding the company. We needed somebody to really help lead the charge on a project, and I knew almost from the outset that he wasn't a good long-term fit for our firm's culture. He didn't really have the same work ethic or ability to resolve issues. In my haste to get someone onboard, I had made an error in judgment during hiring.

He wasn't a good fit culturally, but in the short-term, he had talents that could help get the project set up until we could hand it off to someone else. So we kept him for several months, but at all times, we essentially kept him at arm's length. On some level, this seemed like a very deceptive thing to do, but as the business owner, you have to keep reminding yourself the underlying reason for keeping the person on. In this case, it was because we were growing the business, which would lead to other opportunities for more employees. So there was a greater good for keeping him around at least for the short-term. Plus, as long as someone is actually employed, there's always a chance that they will turn things around and improve. So keeping a poker face in front of that employee leaves the door open for him to become a good employee. But, more often than not, a person who isn't a good fit from the start will remain that way.

In my own experience, it's also necessary to keep that employee somewhat in the dark because if an employee knows that he's not going to be long-term, he's not going to give you his best work.

He'll start looking for other jobs, and he may even look for ways to sandbag the project or extend it even longer.

So unfortunately, the best way to handle this situation is to keep displaying a poker face and continue to do so until you, as the business owner, are ready to make your move.

At the same time, you need to be relentless in your search for someone else to take this person's place. In our case, it was difficult to find an employee to take over the project and who also fit our culture, so we kept the employee that I knew we wanted to let go for a longer period of time.

## Situation 2
## Too Many Projects at Once

A similar situation that could delay letting someone go is when the employee has been with you for a long time, and you do want to let him go, but there are just too many projects on the table to terminate him right now. To the owner's credit, the business is very busy, but the timing is just not right for losing anyone who knows what he's doing.

The strategy is the same as in the previous example: you should be relentlessly looking for someone to take over the position, and you need to keep your poker face and retain that arm's length relationship.

## Situation 3
## Company Morale

The third situation that may delay a termination is really more about the morale of the company. In this one, you've decided that it's time to let somebody go. As far as staffing goes, you're ready to do it. Maybe you're downsizing your company, or maybe you found a suitable replacement right away. But the holidays are coming up, or there's an event coming up, and you want to be very calculated about when you let the person go because you're considering how the other employees might react. You also need to consider your own feelings in this situation.

We had this happen during the holiday season. We realized in early November that our company needed to do a bit of downsizing, but Thanksgiving was coming followed by Christmas and the New Year.

As a business owner, I knew that it would be really challenging to go through the process of letting several people go. Their performance was not as poor as other people who I'd let go. It was more of a numbers issue. On a personal level, I knew it was going to be very stressful for me to go through the act, and I certainly didn't want to drag it out through the holidays. So I made the choice to let them go two weeks before Thanksgiving. You may decide it is better to wait until after the holidays. Each business owner is different, for me I knew it would weigh on me until it was over, whatever serves the business owner best—although it may seem selfish on the surface—is also what serves the business the best.

In another instance, I needed to let an employee go because his performance had changed over time; he was really no longer right for his position. Thanksgiving was fast approaching, so I waited until the holiday was over and let him go the first week of December. He had been with the firm for a while, so I thought it more appropriate for me to tough it out over the holiday and let him enjoy Thanksgiving with his family but then let him go a few weeks before Christmas.

The point is, letting someone go during the holidays impacts everyone. Employees are likely going to go visit their family, and they'll be asked how their life is going, so you want to keep that in mind. But also keep in mind that you're going to have your own holiday with your own family. And you don't want to be distracted and thinking about the horrible termination you have to do on the Monday after Thanksgiving or the day after Christmas, when everyone comes back from the holiday break.

Besides the holidays, a company event is another situation where you should consider the morale of the company. Our firm has a holiday party in the middle of January. Every year, the week before the holiday party, I end up terminating a couple of employees. Although that may seem coldhearted, I would rather stomach the termination before the holiday party than have to go to the party and give out false handshakes and maintain a false smile in front of those soon-to-be-terminated employees, only to terminate them a week or two after the event. So for that, again, I make the decision based on what I can tolerate and what feels most comfortable to me as the business owner.

If you want to keep your company healthy, it's important to remember that you should always hold the interests of the business, the business owner, and the people that drive your business ahead of the people who are holding the business behind. So the business leader's timing trumps everything else.

## REDUCING RISK

Again, every business owner should consult his or her own human resources attorney or internal human resources advisor before terminating an employee. This is an important component to minimize risk.

There's an emotional component to every termination, and the more emotion involved, the more risk for your company. So the more you can reduce that emotion, the more you reduce your risk. If somebody leaves and he's feeling really embarrassed or upset or angry, he's much more likely to seek some form of revenge, whether he hires an attorney, posts really negative information on the Internet, or takes some other action that negatively impacts the company.

The more you can minimize the emotion and allow the person being let go an opportunity to release that emotion, the better. So it's important to be very calculated and to consider how to minimize the emotion of the event in an effort to reduce your risk.

You can also reduce risk by gathering supporting data or information that tracks the employee's poor performance. It is vital, as the business owner, to have some data to support your position and to show that the employee is not performing well. This information not only supports your decision to terminate the employee, but you'll also want to share it with those key employees that you bring into the situation as you set up the termination to logically explain to them why you're making this move.

Most of your key employees are not actual entrepreneurs themselves. They may or may not have management experience, but what makes them key employees is that they are very good workers. Most of the time, they only want two things: they just want to do their job, and for their job to follow a very rational plan and a rational leader who inspires them.

Most employees are not used to being involved in terminating someone or even knowing that someone is being terminated. So when you involve a key employee in the termination of another employee, you can expect him to be more hesitant. He may be a little emotional about the idea, but more importantly, he's going to want to see that you're not doing this termination out of emotion or spite and that there is clear rationale to the act. The data you gather to support the decision to terminate the employee will be your best evidence to gain support from your key employees that you're trying to rally around the act.

As a last-ditch effort before the termination and one last step in reducing risk, it's a good idea to sit down with the employee that you're planning to terminate and discuss the problem with him. You must be very honest and candid with him as you discuss the problem, because part of the goal is to minimize the surprise element when the termination occurs. This meeting occurs after the first strike (verbal) and second strike (written warning) and is part of the third strike (final written warning).

I call this the "come to Jesus meeting," because it's very straight-forward, and it spells out exactly what you expect from the employee by a specified date in the very near future. For example, tell the employee you need to see improvement in areas A, B, and C within two weeks.

Mainly this meeting gets all of your concerns out on the table, and it can be helpful in terms of documenting the process that you're going through. However, while most rational people being told by their boss that they must accomplish certain tasks by a specified time would just do those tasks, in my experience, for a good portion of people, a certain level of defiance kicks in. Some employees even appear to be insulted that you dared to tell them that they are not doing a good job. Unfortunately, I find that the "come to Jesus meeting" usually results in the employee giving the business owner even more reason to terminate the employment.

Still, by using the three-strikes approach before the termination, you can also calm down the good employees in your organization who can see that there is a process that gets followed so that they don't nervously wonder whether they're going to get fired without warning.

## PREPARING FOR THE ACT

The actual act of terminating the employee takes place in a separate room—such as a small conference room. This will be discussed in more detail in the next chapter.

Here, I'd like to discuss what happens beforehand—outside the room. The below actions will help guide you through protecting your company when you are terminating an employee who has access to sensitive information—everything from security codes to confidential customer data.

There are several areas of concern that you need to pay close attention to if you decide to terminate an employee, particularly if the person you are letting go is a key employee, such as a department leader.

### Area 1
### Information Technology

When you are letting go an employee who has access your company's computer systems containing sensitive information, you must always prioritize removing their access. The best thing to do is talk to whoever leads your IT department. Let them know what, when, and where you are letting the employee go, and arrange for IT to block or disable the employee's access during or immediately after you terminate the employee.

However, if you're letting your IT person go, he has access to your entire server and all of your electronic information. If you're not a very tech-savvy business owner, it can be really nerve-racking to let somebody go who you depend on for your company's technical information.

In this situation, you can hire an outside IT vendor to be ready to take full control as soon as the IT lead is gone. You can accomplish this by making the excuse that you need to bolster your company's IT capabilities for a while. Then have that vendor review all the ways you can properly protect your security while looking for someone else to fill the IT leader's role. The outside IT vendor can also ensure that your IT is buttoned-down and as safe as possible as soon as the IT leader has been terminated. You may also need to ask this vendor or another independent vendor to help you find another IT leader.

# Area 2
# Accounting Department

Another area that is especially nerve-racking for a business owner to deal with when terminating employees is the accounting department. For example, we had an accounting manager who wasn't doing her job, and she was doing a lot of things that company owners dread. We knew we had to let her go, but she had full access to money and to accounts. Especially if you're a business owner that is not very numbers savvy and not very interested in accounting, this can be a particularly nerve-racking situation to be in.

Here again, the best thing to do is to hire an independent firm. Have an independent CPA firm begin by reviewing your books just to start to make some sort of contact with your firm in a business way. Then have the firm do some deeper investigation of your books to ensure that everything is in order and that you're prepared to terminate a key person from your accounting department.

Once you're assured that your accounting is in order, then you need to be prepared to act very quickly. When you terminate the person, you need to immediately let the banks know that you are letting him go and that his access is revoked.

Before we let a key person in our accounting department go, we met with all of our banks, we met with her replacement, and we met with our outside CPA. We investigated all of her actions so that the day we let her go, we were able to revoke all of her authorization and transfer her tasks. We also advised a few clients that we were going to be changing leadership in that department, so if there were any issues, they should contact us, the business owners, rather than someone else in the accounting department.

## Area 3
## Client Information

Another situation that is very challenging is when the employee being let go is privy to sensitive client information.

One time, I let an employee go who had formed a relationship with a key client. I terminated the employee by being direct, professional, and candid.

Two months later, while I was out of the office at a conference, he called our client directly and complained about me and how I ran the firm. Ultimately, I talked to the client and explained the situation: that this was an employee who was terminated, and he had some ill feelings about it—that we were doing everything we could, but the situation was really not our fault. The point is that employees who are terminated may use their access to your clients to try to hurt you. But this should not prevent you from taking the action that you should take—which is terminating an employee when the need arises. From the above example, you can see that this employee tried to hurt my business. But I have never regretted parting ways. A reasonable person understands that a terminated employee is often a biased person.

Proactively, you want to be very guarded with who in your company has the information needed to communicate with clients, particularly your top customers. It's very tempting with high-maintenance clients to allow several employees communication with the client because they can resolve all the small issues that help you function. But you should be very guarded in who you bring into that inner circle, even if it allows your company to operate more efficiently and prevents you, the owner, from being dragged down into the day-to-day operations.

Once an employee who has left your company chooses to contact your client, it's best to be upfront with your client—should that conversation result in a call to your offices. Keep that conversation with your client honest, but the less said the better. Tell your client that you, unfortunately, had to let that person go, but for legal reasons, you can't really get into specifics. Most of the time, the client will then realize he is dealing with a disgruntled employee, and he will respect you for protecting the former employee's rights.

Whatever you do, avoid a back and forth with your client about the dirty details. Your client doesn't want that, and he certainly doesn't want to view you as a gossiper. That would be a little like watching two friends or a married couple argue and expecting him to pick a side. But instead of him thinking you're right and your ex-employee is wrong, he's likely just to think you're both a little wacky.

Take the high road, and remain professional when dealing with any issues that arise as a result of such a negative experience.

## ADVANCE DOCUMENTATION AND PREPARATIONS

Before executing the act of terminating someone, you should always create a sequence of events to cover all aspects of the act itself. In chapter 5, I'll talk more about the steps leading up to the termination along with what happens inside the conference room, but here I want to stress some of the early preparation pieces.

One of the critical early steps is that the IT department must be prepared to immediately change the person's security or clearance. During the act of terminating the employee, someone from IT must be ready to disable the soon-to-be terminated employee's access from your company's systems. If you have a team that's accustomed to this kind of situation, there won't be an emotional reaction to the act.

Second, I always have another employee on hand in case there is a need for physical security.

Third, any time you offer a severance (and I don't always offer one), you should always seek a release in exchange. The release and severance offer must be in writing and prepared in advance. The smoothest and least painful approach is to simply put the document in front of the employee and explain it. This usually avoids uncomfortable follow-up conversations and arguments. I cannot stress it enough, you want to avoid follow-ups if possible, you want to be done. In addition to the performance evaluation log that I discussed earlier, your human resources department—or you, as the business owner—need to prepare the documentation that is required for the termination. Your ultimate goal is to be done with this situation and back to working on making your company profitable. You don't want to carry this action with you emotionally. So your goal needs to be to have the termination conversation in one shot and be done with the action.

You should also have any severance pay already decided and the paperwork already prepared. I recommend that a business owner offer two to four weeks of severance. As part of one of the most challenging terminations I've done, I offered ten weeks of pay as a severance. It was early on in my career, and I was close with the employee. To help mentally accept that I was going to go through with the termination, I decided it would be easier on me if I gave him a bigger severance; I felt it would release my guilt. But if you're a small business owner, that is an enormous amount of money for an employee who's not going to give you any production. Almost immediately following that termination I regretted it.

So you may decide to give a bigger severance the first time you terminate someone in order to help get you over the emotional hurdle of deciding to go through with what you know in your gut is the right decision. Otherwise, as I said, I recommend two to four weeks of a person's pay as the severance package, and then ask for a release in return. The reasoning is simple: if you're going to pay somebody, you need to get something in return, and a release is it.

You can find several examples of releases online, but you should consult with your human resources attorney to review my document or anything taken from the Internet to ensure it complies with your state-specific laws.

Having all your paperwork ready before you enter the termination conference room reduces any back-and-forth negotiation or follow-up conversations.

We'll discuss this further in chapter 5, but remember this: when you go into the room, as the business owner, you actually have the most control of the conversation. This is the best time to present the paperwork you prepared and approved.

Having your paperwork prepared in advance also aids you in dealing with Equal Employment Opportunity Commission (EEOC) issues. These issues—as well as any other legalities—are especially important to cover with your attorney. In the state of Washington where I do work, if a person is over age 40, he has a certain amount of extra time to review his release and severance agreement. So the employee that is being let go must sign and return the document at a later date; signing it in the room won't suffice.

## WHEN TO POST THE JOB OPENING

Earlier I mentioned the three-strike process (fourth strike, you're out), which is a warning system to give the employee a heads-up that you're dissatisfied with his performance and to reduce your risk.

Often, by the time the last warning is given, the soon-to-be-vacant job should be posted in various places in an early effort to find the employee's replacement. This is not always the case, but the goal here is to minimize the gap in job coverage. Later in the book I'll expand on the effect of timing the replacement of a terminated employee on other members of the team. But for now, here are three scenarios I typically follow when placing an ad:

# Scenario 1
## Posting an Ad for a General Position

If the job is an entry-level position or a general one, like grocery clerk, store clerk, administrative assistant, or waiter at a restaurant, go ahead and post your job so that the moment the person is terminated, you can have his replacement starting the day after or soon thereafter. Posting a job for a general position is not going to raise any suspicions. These jobs are posted all the time, and you'll be able to bring in several candidates without raising suspicions. By posting the job in advance of the termination, you can have a replacement in as quickly as possible and reduce how much business you're going to lose.

I've done this dozens of times; it allows me to have a replacement in place within a few days. And I've never really had an issue with this practice. But one time I did experience an awkward moment where a lazy employee in a position that was somewhat specialized came to me and announced that he had seen the ad and was glad we were hiring another person for the team because everybody was so busy trying to keep up with all the work.

I was kind of embarrassed that he had seen the ad, because it was really for his replacement. But then I realized that not only was he not doing good work for me, but he was also looking for another job himself, and that's why he found the ad. It certainly solidified my desire to let him go.

# Scenario 2
# Replacing a Key Role

Another situation is when you have a person in a key role, such as a manager, and he's just not right for the position. Maybe he isn't getting enough work done, or he doesn't have the right attitude, or the role is just too challenging. But it's too specific of a role to run an ad before you terminate the employment.

Unfortunately, sometimes the only way to handle this is to let the manager go before hiring a replacement. I've done this and just told his team that I had to let the manager go and I don't have a replacement, so as the business owner, I would have to pitch in for the short-term. Then I immediately began looking for a replacement.

The upside to this situation is that when you have a manager or an employee in a specialized role and he's not a good fit, the people who work most closely with him usually already know that. Often, they would rather this person was let go and replaced. So when you come to them and tell them honestly that you need to replace the manager and that you don't have a replacement for him yet, you come across to your team as having made the right choice while also being human about it. Often, your other key people will pitch in and give you a little extra effort, and you'll end up not losing as much work or business as you were afraid you might.

This method works best with key personnel and management-type roles. Entry-level roles typically don't have enough stake in the company for anyone to really try to pitch in, so you might as well have another person lined up. But for specialized roles, you can get a little bit of extra effort out of the team around that person if you come to the team, hat in hand, and just explain that you really didn't have a choice or a better plan.

## Scenario 3
## Using a Vendor

Another way to deal with terminating a key employee, such as a manager, is to hire an outside vendor (headhunter) to search for a replacement while you're waiting to terminate the unproductive employee. This allows you to have interviews going on at an outside location during the termination process.

I have had mixed results using these types of vendors. As the owner of a small business, you usually have a very strong sense of how you want the job done and what kind of personality you want to fill the role. As I mentioned earlier in the book, I have a sense of what energy works best with mine and what kind of person works best. And you want a key employee to definitely be somebody who works really well with you and fits your vision.

So using an outside company can present some challenges when that firm doesn't really have a great understanding of your vision or your energy and what you're looking for in a key person. However, an outside vendor can find a group of candidates and whittle the selections down to five or ten interviews and then maybe set those up for you to conduct at an off-site location.

As a business leader, it's rarely easy to let someone go, and in many cases, it can seem like a callous, inhumane act. From my standpoint, the human decency comes from keeping a healthy company; it comes from keeping good employees happy and well-compensated, and it comes from keeping your company in a position to survive in the long term so that your good employees can count on their position for a long time.

When it comes to letting somebody go who is totally letting me and the company down because he's not getting the job done or has a bad attitude that's affecting others, it's really tough for me to be swayed by the human component. I do tend to think almost entirely in black and white in terms of the business owner, the leader, and what's in the best interests of the company and its workers.

However, I am a big believer in minimizing the emotional situation. It is important to remember that there is a certain tarnish about going through with a dramatic act like terminating employment around the holidays. Oftentimes, terminations are not performance-based—they're actually a company doing downsizing, which may mean you're eliminating an entire department, including some employees who really did give a good effort. It's just a numbers situation. You don't need five people in a certain position anymore, now you only need three. In that case, I think it is really important to be as decent about the termination process as possible.

# Chapter 3 Takeaways

1} A checklist of documents and elements to prepare in advance:

- Choose a place, day, and time.

- Have IT prepared to remove ex-employee's access.

- Have accounting review accounts and client files.

- Performance evaluation log.

- Separation paperwork, including optional severance package.

- A time line for how the termination is expected to go.

- A termination script for inside the room.

- A list of the company property that the employee needs to return.

- A list of any outstanding expenses that need to be settled.

- A proposed action plan for the employee to gather personal items or to ship items if extensive.

- A strategy for what to tell coworkers after the termination is over.

- Explanation for clients if appropriate.

# CHAPTER
# 4

## BUILDING YOUR RESOLVE

A big piece of the termination process for the leader is to overcome the emotions and prepare himself to do the actual act.

To do this, the leader has to make the decision whether or not this person should be let go, if he just needs to be confronted, or if, as a business owner, you're not being fair to him because you're not providing him some sort of resource to succeed. The first issue is to make the decision that terminating the employee is the right thing to do. Second, the business leader has to overcome the emotions of having to let someone go. You have to clear your mind of the emotions. Until you've cleared your mind of those emotions, you will not know if you made the right choice.

In doing this, there are five stages of emotions that the business leader must overcome. These stages are, at their core, analogous to the five stages of grief modeled by Swiss psychiatrist Elisabeth Kübler-Ross in her book *On Death and Dying* and are commonly known as denial, anger, bargaining, depression, and acceptance. I like to refer to them as the *five stages of building resolve.*

If you are a business leader who is trained in letting people go—you've had some experience at letting people go and maybe even developed some skill or a few techniques over time—then the goal when you realize you have a problem employee is to go right to acceptance of the situation and then move on to deciding that termination is the right choice.

But the untrained leader—the business professional who hasn't had a lot of experience terminating employees—will almost always have to work through all five stages of resolve before he can actually get to a place where he decides that this is the right choice. Here are those five stages:

1. *Denial. The "I don't think I actually have to let this person go" stage.* Deciding to terminate an employee always starts out with questioning whether a person should be dismissed from the job. If the employee has missed deadlines or not shown up for work, or he's let you down somehow—or worse—he's gone behind your back over an issue or done something damaging to the company, something has happened to raise the question to you, the leader, of what should be done about the situation.

   In my experience, without proper training, a leader won't want to confront the problem. With anything that occurs in business that's damaging to the company, the first reaction for the untrained leader is denial—he may make excuses for it, or he may even arrange work-arounds. In fact, business leaders have told me many times that they have a problem employee, but everyone just "works around it." What that actually translates to is a lot of other people who aren't functioning within the realms of their own jobs but who instead are having to take on some sort of expanded role in order to accommodate the issue of how this one individual is letting the company down.

So I see a lot of denial, and in my experience working with other leaders, this is the hardest piece for a leader—deciding to confront the situation. As you work through the issue, keep in mind that you don't have to decide to let the person go, but you owe it to the company to confront the situation

*Remember: being logical or rational rather than emotional will allow you to accept the termination as the right choice, and the less energy you spend on an emotional response or denial, the better.*

There have been a lot of instances in my career when I wanted to avoid confronting the issue. But overcoming that denial is the first stage of deciding to let somebody go, and all you have to do to address it is to just mentally say, "There is an issue here, something is not working correctly in my company, and I need to confront it." You're not deciding to let the person go—you're deciding to confront the issue. When you decide to confront, it you're releasing the denial stage.

2. *Anger. The "I hate this situation" stage.* The thought of letting someone go makes many business leaders angry. They just hate everything about the idea.

Anyone who operates a business successfully knows that one of the greatest joys in running a company is creating opportunities for employees. It's not only about creating a better company, but it's also about improving peoples' lives, especially key employees whose lives are better because of the position that you created. In truth, it's actually very painful to work hard, create a position, and then have somebody let you down because he is not up for the role.

So once a business owner admits there's a problem, and he confronts the issue, the next stage of the process is anger. He's angry that he has to confront this person. He's angry at the person for letting him down. He's angry that the situation got to where it is in the first place. Angry that the work isn't getting done. Sometimes he just has a short fuse and may lash out at anyone that stops by his office.

The anger stage is what damages a lot of partnerships. Typically, at first, one partner is ready to talk about the problem, and the other one is in denial, so he doesn't want to talk about it. An untrained partner, who is typically the one still in denial, has to work his way through all the five stages of building resolve, while the partner who has dealt with a similar situation will immediately go to the last stage, the acceptance stage, and be ready to start talking about the logistics of whether a termination is the correct step to take. If you are in a partnership and your partner shows anger while discussing a termination, do not take the anger personally. Your partner is probably less comfortable with terminating employees than you. They are working through the process so that they can accept it. Talk to them dispassionately, making logical points. Then come back after you give them time to process it and present yourself in the same dispassionate tone with logical points.

Employees have a different mind-set than the owner. They don't typically see things from the same point of view, so sometimes one of them will let you down. He'll be more interested in his own paycheck than in the company's profitability. He'll be more interested in time off than in company deadlines. During work, while being paid by the owner, an employee can be more concerned with issues outside of work than with the work itself.

But if you acknowledge thatan employee is never going to be you, the business owner, and he's going to have limitations that you don't have, as the business owner, then you can release your anger and get on with making a decision about whether he's doing the job he's been employed to do. Yes, his level of dedication may be disappointing, but can he do the job?

3. *Bargaining. The "If only . . . " stage.* This stage is the one stage a lot of business leaders really struggle with. They think, "Well, if only we had trained him better," or "If only we gave him more resources," or "If only we gave him more people," or "If only we were more accepting." But if the employee legitimately has the skills for the job, then he can do the job that he's been hired to do. If not, there is someone else out there who is willing to do the job that the person currently in the role is unwilling to do. The only reason that you're in this

conversation in your head or with your partner is because that employee is not getting the job done.

Some of the takeaways when you're bargaining over the issue may, in truth, be fair discussions about how to improve your company. Even a sophisticated, trained mind that goes right to the last stage, the acceptance stage, can still go back to the emotions of doubt and anxiety. If that happens, he may even decide to give the employee two weeks to correct himself. But often the untrained business leader is going to be stuck in a bargaining stage. The danger here is that this stage can go on indefinitely. There's always another way to help somebody get better at his job. The reality is that the employee is probably not going to get better, so it's important to get beyond the bargaining stage as quickly as possible.

A good way to quickly bypass bargaining is to just ask yourself, "If I gave the same amount of resources to another person out there, could he get the job done?" If the answer is yes, then you want to move through the remaining emotions or stages that I have listed here as quickly as possible so you can really get down to the question of whether this person is the right fit. What's the logic and reasoning behind your decision?

4.  *Depression. The letdown stage.* After moving through the other stages, rather than just getting on with acceptance and making a logical decision, the untrained business leader will become depressed. In the business setting, if you're not aware of it, the depression can settle in and stay for a long time, keeping you from reaching the acceptance stage.

This can be very damaging, especially if it lingers for months and months. It can drain the enthusiasm and life out of a company waiting on the business leader to be ready to act. You, as the business owner, are damaging your company when you allow yourself to linger in depression.

So the key is to own the issue: acknowledge it and say, yes, this person did let me down and it is sad, but I am going to get past this.

One of the tricks I have for getting past depression in a business setting is to bring the issue back to why I'm running a company in the first place. What joy do I get out of owning my own company, and who does my company serve?

For me, my company serves my family. It serves my mind, my goals, and my ambitions. It serves my good employees, and it serves my clients.

It also allows me to do things in my community that I otherwise couldn't do if I simply worked a nine-to-five job. When I bring my mind back to all the good things that my company does, and that the reason I'm having to confront this issue is because there's damage being done to my company, it moves me out of depression pretty quickly.

So a trained business mind can move through the stages and do an analysis quickly and get on to the last stage of the emotions of letting somebody go, which is acceptance.

5. *Acceptance. The logic and strategy stage.* When you accept that you have to let someone in your company go, you can begin

to figure out the logic and the strategy of the termination. Once my nerves are calmed down, and I've moved through the stages and am in acceptance mode, I can start thinking about the best way to move forward.

Now you have to actually confront the situation and create a strategy. As I mentioned in an earlier chapter, I do an exercise where, on a piece of paper, I list the position title and then I write down all the things that position could ideally do— what problems would the position solve, the ideas it would create, and what it would produce. I also list the personality or attitude I'd like to see in that position, and I write down what I'm willing to pay for this position if I could find a person to fulfill all the responsibilities I have outlined.

I don't put any names on the paper because the more I can objectively think in terms of the position, the more easily I can avoid emotional pitfalls.

Then I go down the list and ask myself if the employee in question is really up to the task. How many of the items on the list is the employee doing, and how many is he not doing?

Once I've written it out on paper, the answer is almost always clear. Usually, I can look at what I've written on the paper and detach myself from the situation and pretty quickly see that either this person's not a good fit and he's not giving me what I need, or he actually gives me a lot of what I need but is weak in some areas. In that case, maybe I just need to have a hard conversation with him, but I don't necessarily have to let him go. Or maybe the problem is more my fault, which sends me back to that bargaining stage but in a logical and unemotional way to determine if what's needed is a matter of additional resources.

This exercise is a great way to detach yourself from the situation, move through the emotions, get right to acceptance, and come to the right decision that makes sense for your company.

Another exercise I use when I'm trying to build my resolve is I go outside. For example, I like to go out to the roof of the parking garage next to my building.

Up there, I just look up at the sky and I think: the sky is so huge, the universe is so huge, there's so much industry under this sky, there are so many huge buildings, and so many people, and my problem today is actually a lot smaller than I really thought it was. I was thinking about it as a life-changing problem, but really, in comparison to everything that's out there, I can realize it's much smaller than that. There's a world of opportunity out there, and it's a pretty fair bet that this person that is being let go will connect with some of that.

This exercise helps me build up my resolve and get more clarity so that I can move forward.

## THE ART OF CONFRONTATION

Now that you have worked through the various stages, you're on to building up your resolve to have the conversation. Many successful business owners are energy people. We get a lot done. We can think really fast. We can make competent decisions without all the information. We're very confident.

But what's difficult for some business owners—and is not a trait everyone possesses—is the skill of confrontation. What I learned through a lot of practice is that the art of confrontation can not only help you get through letting somebody go in a very professional and humane way, but it also can help you avoid letting people go because you are able to have those tough love conversations before the situation gets to a breaking point.

It's taken me a lot of years and a lot of situations to really hone my skill for the art of confrontation. I've learned that there are two key pieces to confrontation.

First of all, the art of confrontation really starts with being able to matter-of-factly tell someone the truth. It's not yelling. It's not anger. Many people misconstrue the idea of a confrontational personality as someone who yells and screams, while a person who is more stoic is someone who avoids confrontation. Being very vocal actually hurts you as a business owner because it takes logical conversations to an emotional level. In order to have a logical solution and get to a result, you need to avoid emotions.

Being able to matter-of-factly tell someone the truth is key: "You're late, and that doesn't work," or "You missed this deadline, and if it happens again, then I'm going to have to look seriously at whether or not this position is too much for you," or "Your quotas are down." Whatever needs to be said to somebody, it's very important that you say it truthfully and in a matter-of-fact voice. Ultimately, the truth is that the business is being damaged, and now you have to do something about it.

The second piece to confrontation is to always meet in private. When you're letting somebody go, obviously, you're going to build up more strategy and work through the steps that I talked about in previous chapters. But any confrontational conversation in advance of the actual termination should also be done in private; this includes any conversation in which you're candidly pointing out how the employee is letting you down. When you have a conversation in public, people tend to get embarrassed. And when they are embarrassed, they tend to do two things—lash out and defend themselves. When they lash out, they can't hear what you're saying, and it causes a big disturbance in your company. And when they're defensive, they're not accepting what you're saying; they're trying to tell you all the reasons you're wrong.

Take the employee into a private room and speak to him matter-of-factly from the perspective of the business owner. You should always have a witness—a human resources person or a trusted leader in the room during this conversation. If the employee you're speaking with has any respect at all for you, then he should listen and take it all in. If he doesn't listen and take it in, then he's not a good fit for your company. The fact that he doesn't respect you is a sign that something is amiss. He's not going to give you what you need and want, and he's someone you should let go.

If he's giving you a very positive reaction, nodding his head and maybe taking notes, these are signs that he's going to turn things around and get the job done. Caution: Head nodding and note taking notes could also be lip service, and he could go right back to doing things the same old way, so never be too proud of yourself as a business owner for having a confrontational meeting with someone who appears to be very agreeable. The proof is always in the pudding.

It's reflected in the employee's work. Always give the employee a deadline for turning things around.

Once you're accepting of the truth of your situation, then you will use logic and strategy to resolve it, and you have developed all of the skills there are for building your resolve in letting somebody go. At this point you simply have to decide to do it, and then do it.

## COMING OUT OF THE ACT

If, by now, you think you're going to feel great after everything's done, you're not. So far, we've talked about building your resolve prior to the act. Afterward, you're still going to have some anxiety, and you're still going to have some questions. But now you can be better prepared.

In the next chapter, I'll talk about the actual act of letting someone go. After you've done that, you will still need to work through some emotions. Here are some pointers to help you rebuild your resolve.

## EXAMINE YOUR EMOTIONS

Initially, once you've left the room and the person has left the premises, you'll need to examine your emotions. Do you feel better? Are you feeling worse? For me, even though I've written down what I want from a position and found that the person in that position is never going to be a good fit, I still find the act of terminating him to be really tough. But as soon as he's out the door, I always feel better. I always feel like I have advanced the company.

It may be a sad time for a little while. There may be some tough work ahead, and I may have to take on extra work. But I always feel a sense of advancing the company toward the goal of being a better company. Let's face it, hiring is fun, and terminating is no fun. So hiring and training a new person may result in a whole new set of growing pains, and it may be some time before the new person is producing what you need. But the hard part is over. Now you've reached the part that's a little more enjoyable.

## NO REGRETS, NO DOUBTS

After a termination, a business owner may have regret or doubt about whether it was the right decision. I almost never have regret about letting somebody go because usually, by now, I have reached a place where I have released the emotions. I've analyzed the situation. I have a logical conclusion and that conclusion has played itself out. Now it's about trying to get on with having a better company, so I don't really have regret. Instead, as I've said, what I usually feel is relief.

Most business owners are people who are used to taking risks. We are used to putting ourselves out there. When you try something and it doesn't work out—it's not that damaging, and you just move on. You learn, you go on to the next thing, and you try to get better. What's more damaging to an entrepreneur is a situation where you're not able to take the risk. You can't move forward. To me, it's actually harder to have an opportunity to advance my company but not be able to go forward with it.

I don't think most of the entrepreneurs I know have much regret. They may not like confrontation. They may go through the five stages of building resolve when deciding to confront the question of whether to let somebody go. But once they've let that person go, then I think most entrepreneurs are ready to move on and get back to business.

However, doubt is another issue that some business leaders face after letting someone go. Obviously, when we go through the five stages of building resolve, there's a lot of doubt that could enter into the situation because of the emotions involved. But even after the act is done, you could have doubts about the strategy that you put in place.

The way I handle doubt is by looking at my company as an ever-evolving thing. It's always trying to get better, so I don't spend a lot of time doubting if a strategy does or doesn't work. If it's not working, then I just tweak it and move forward. I think that resonates with a lot of entrepreneurs because, again, that's how we think. We just tweak and move forward.

Doubt is often felt after terminating somebody. It's realistic to question whether the strategy was the right one to use in that situation. But I don't really label the feeling I have after a termination as doubt. I prefer to look at it as another piece of the problem that needs a solution.

## IT'S REALLY ABOUT THE BOTTOM LINE

Without seeming callous, it's important to remember that letting someone go is really about the bottom line. Everything else is just emotions. And your resolve about the matter really does come down to you deciding that this is the right thing to do.

Again, I always bring myself back to the reasons I have a company: my family, my dreams, my ambitions, my employees that are doing a good job, and my community. Thinking about that really helps me move forward.

Another thing that helps me is recognizing that the person who is letting you down is also preventing a potentially good employee from having a job at your company. Your company is a well-run company that is creating opportunities for people, and someone out there deserves that opportunity.

I remember being riddled with anxiety the last semester of law school because I was clerking at a law firm that wasn't going to hire me. Without a job practicing law, I would be saddled with a lot of student loans and would have to find some other way to pay them back. Meanwhile, I had a fellow student who was clerking at another firm and was going to be hired there. She repeatedly talked in class about how much she didn't care about the job she was being offered but that she was going to take it anyway because of the higher-than-average salary.

It really irritated me because I wanted my own job, and I wasn't getting my opportunity, and here was somebody who was totally taking a position for granted. I thought I was a better attorney than her, I thought I could do a better job than her, and I would have taken the job at half the salary the company was going to pay. I commented in class once about how upset I was that I wasn't getting the job where I clerked, to which she responded that she wouldn't work for the pay I was willing to accept, so I didn't need to feel so bad. I don't know if she was trying to pick up my spirits by putting down the job that I wanted, but the whole situation really upset me and has remained with me throughout my career.

The lesson here? That for every person who is taking the position you have for granted—who is working for your company and doesn't want the job—there is someone out there who can probably do the job better, for less money, and who is looking for work and just needs to be offered the opportunity.

Remember this when you're building up your resolve to go through with a termination. Remember that you're trying to better your company not just for you but for all the other reasons—your family, your goals, your good employees, and your community. And remember that you're creating an opportunity for somebody who is hungry and will appreciate the position.

I've had to terminate a lot of people, and thankfully, a number of those times I hired a second person that appreciated the position a lot more and contributed to the firm a lot more. The change is beneficial for my company, for the employee, for my field, and for my community.

# Chapter 4 Takeaways

1} Five Ways to Overcome Doubt

- Confront the situation: You have worked through the various stages of deciding to terminate. Confronting the situation helps you let someone go in a professional, humane way

- Come out of the act: Realize you aren't going to immediately feel great after everything's done. There will still be anxiety and self-questioning—but you are prepared.

- Examine your emotions: After the terminated person has left, evaluate yourself and the situation. Do you feel better—relieved? Or do you feel worse? Usually, even though the act of terminating is incredibly tough, it leaves a person with some relief.

- Make no room for regret and doubt: You have already reached a place where you have released all the emotion. The situation has been analyzed, and the right choice for the well-being of the company and the employee has been made.

- Remember the bottom line: Letting someone go is all about what's best for the company's health—everything else is just emotions. You have resolved to do the right thing, and this will make your company healthier.

# CHAPTER
# 5

## HOW TO HAVE THE DIFFICULT CONVERSATION

Congratulations. You made a decision to move your company forward. Now you have to execute it. The goal of actually going through with the termination is to minimize your risk and to minimize the drama of the situation. Not only do you want as little risk as possible in terms of a potential lawsuit, but you also want to make the actual interruption to your business as insignificant as possible.

As I mentioned earlier, it is critical to reduce the amount of emotion in the situation because that really reduces the amount of risk. The more you rely on your data, the better formulated the strategy and the process that you're going to use, the less emotional you'll be, and the less emotion there will be generated by the situation.

In this chapter, I'm going to lay out how to prepare for the actual act of terminating someone in a professional way.

First, you need to decide the best time of the day and day of the week to let someone go. Remember that, as the employer, letting someone go should be on your time. What time of day makes sense for you as the employer? Think about it: It's the day of the act. You're nervous, you have anxiety, and you're thinking about how it's going to unfold.

For me, depending on the employee and the situation, there are essentially three categories that shape what time of day I'm going to terminate the employment.

## Category 1
## The Standard Employee

While no termination is straightforward; each has its own nuances. But the majority of terminations of standard employees are going to fall into the category of following the recommendations of the experts.

The experts say you should let somebody go toward the end of the day, later in the week. Don't make the employee come in on a Monday morning after a weekend. Do the termination on a Wednesday, Thursday, or Friday, around two or three o'clock in the afternoon.

Unless there's a reason why an employee fits into one of the other two categories I'm going to talk about, most of the time it makes sense to let your termination occur in the middle of the afternoon and in the middle of or later in the week.

## Category 2
## The Scene Maker

The second category is the employee you expect to cause some sort of a scene. You think he's going to be dramatic, he'll be emotional, and he may even be defiant. With these employees, you want the actual event to occur late in the day after as many people as possible have gone home for the day.

For example, several people who knew that we were going to let one employee go had advised me that they were very confident she was going to make a scene, that she would cry, and that she would be defiant. If she got to go back to her desk after she was terminated, she might make a lot of noise slamming furniture and other items.

So we made the decision to do the termination at 5:30 p.m. because she worked a little later than some of the other shifts. Luckily, we ended up not having a scene. But the planning was to do the act as late as possible, so that if anything did happen—if her voice was raised or if she was a little bit more demonstrative at her desk—as few people were in the office as possible.

## Category 3
## High Anxiety

The third category of termination is the one that, for whatever reason, just causes you a lot of anxiety. Maybe the employee won't be super confrontational, but you just carry a stomach-churning degree of anxiety, and the thought of working with him all day and interacting with him is just awful. Or maybe you know the termination is going to be really devastating to that employee. He has a mortgage, or maybe there's an illness in the family. For whatever the reason, it's not a standard termination, and it's giving you a lot of anxiety.

With these employees, I prefer to do the termination as soon as the day begins. If the employee comes in earlier in the day, for example, 8:00 a.m., I'll come in at 6:00 a.m. or 7:00 a.m. just so I'm prepared and ready to handle the termination as as possible.

The idea here is that, during the day, the employee is going to distract you and make you so uncomfortable while you're interacting with him that you're not going to be productive at your own job, and you're going to end up losing money as an employer or losing a production day as a company because you're so distracted with what could occur.

Therefore, you just want to get the termination done as early as possible in the day. This is much more important, and healthier for the business, than trying to wait until the end of the day at the end of the week.

I've had to terminate a few high-level managers on Monday morning, and it caused me anxiety all weekend. I had made the decision on Friday or over the weekend to do the termination, so the plan was to let the person go first thing on Monday morning at 8:00 a.m. Rather than wait until that standard time of late in the day on Thursday and work with this individual all week and suffer through the anxiety while I'm trying to work, I prefer to just come in early and get the termination done as early in the day as possible.

In these instances, as soon as the manager arrived at 7:30 a.m. or 8:00 a.m., I was prepared to let him go and be done with the task, so I could get on with my week and have as productive a week after the fact, as possible.

The bottom line is the termination really doesn't have to happen on a certain day or even a certain time of day. It should just occur as soon after you make the decision as possible because you're carrying so much anxiety.

## BUILDING CONFIDENCE

A key piece to getting ready for the termination is building your own confidence before entering the room where the termination will occur.

The most important thing to remember is that, as the employer, you were in a logical place when you decided this was the right move.

The day of the termination, it's totally normal to have a lot of nerves and to let those nerves—along with fear—distract you and become somewhat of a devil's advocate, posing questions such as, "Am I sure I want to do this?" and "But didn't he do a good job on that one project?" These are just a couple of the questions that will permeate your thoughts.

Remember that you examined all the data, gave the employee chances, performed all the necessary procedures to reduce risk, and now the decision has been made. And that decision was made based on rational thinking combined with your gut feeling as a business owner. Again, you've already decided that this was going to occur. Any thoughts and second-guessing you're having should be recognized as coming from a place of anxiety and not a place of rational thought.

Once you have accepted that the decision is final, then your resolve should carry you through the entire process. It will affect your tone of voice in the room, it will affect how you respond to any defensive posturing from the employee, and it will affect how you interact with other employees who you might bring in on the process.

But that determination that you are going to do this termination and that an irreversible decision has been made will help bring not only your own confidence up but also help you execute the process the best you possibly can.

## SETTING UP THE ROOM

As I briefly mentioned earlier, the termination itself should take place in a room. Ideally, this should be a small conference room or other neutral setting, if possible, away from the larger work area.

There are five steps to setting this room up for the termination:

1. *The physical area.* The first step in setting up the selected room is arranging the physical area. You may use your own office or another office, but I have a conference room that I use. Whatever space you choose, just have a designated area where the conversation and termination is going to occur.

   Since I use a conference room, I pull down all the shades that go to windows outside of the conference room so people who walk by can't look in, which eliminates distractions. I also make sure that any documents or items that could be taken or used in anger are removed from the room and that it has a very clean, uncluttered appeal.

   In addition, I make sure that there are tissues in the room because a lot of people end up crying and feeling emotional when this occurs.

Whatever works for you as the employer, whether it's in your office, an off-site location, or in your own conference room, you want to make sure that you've reviewed the room a few minutes ahead of time and that it is situated and arranged in a way that will make you the most comfortable.

2. *Identify other parties.* The second step of setting up the situation is to identify who else will be in the know about the termination. Talk to the least amount of people who need to know. In my company, I usually end up having five people who know. In addition to me and my partner, our human resources person, our IT person, and the supervisor of the employee. Often, I have one other trusted advisor who I've talked to ahead of time, and he's given me good counsel to make sure that I saw the situation clearly and that I was clear on my decision.

   Not every business owner will have five people that he consults, but it is a good idea to make sure that you consult at least one extra, third party to help you feel clear on your decision. As mentioned previously, it's important to discuss any termination with either a human resources attorney that you subcontract or the head of your human resources department. Again, the supervisor should also be in the loop.

3. *Discuss the plan of action.* I have always required that a second person be in the room with me when I terminate someone. If a man is being terminated, that second person is a man. From my own experience, it's highly inadvisable to have two women in the room when terminating a man. My partner, wife, once

did this and when the employee became very hostile, it was a scary situation for her and the other female in the room.

After you decide who the other person in the room will be, you should meet with them. I have an independent conversation with that person that's more in-depth about what we think will happen, what we're going to say, how the act will unfold, and our plan of action. We go over the steps of who's going to do the talking (which will be me) and who's going to get the employee from his desk (the other person). We also confirm that the IT department is ready to remove that employee's access as soon as he leaves his desk to come to the conference room.

4. *Being prepared.* The ultimate responsibility of the person who is letting someone go is to be as prepared as possible. Therefore, it's important for me as the business owner to have the statements I'm going to say written out in advance so that I have my position rehearsed and ready to be said as smoothly as possible. As I mentioned in chapter three, I also need to have any reports ready, the termination agreement ready to be signed, any severance paperwork I want signed, a list of the company property that the employee needs to return, and any outstanding expenses that need to be settled.

5. *The walk.* Once the documentation, the room, and the parties involved are ready, the next step is the act of walking and retrieving the employee being terminated. This is like the switch that makes me ready to do the conversation.

Until I'm in the room, I need some space to prepare. For me personally, it's really awkward and uncomfortable to walk casually up to someone at their desk when he's surrounded by his peers or working on a project, and say, "Hey, can I talk to you in the conference room?" So I always have the second person go get the employee that we're going to terminate. I quickly confirm with IT that we're ready to terminate the employee access—sometimes this is just eye contact on the way to the room—so that when the act is finished, if the employee goes back to his desk, he will be locked out and cannot access any files. Then I walk to the conference room.

Since we handle a lot of sensitive information in my business, it is critical that once we have decided that an employee is no longer a good fit, and we let him know, he must leave the premises right then and there. He's not allowed to touch any other files.

My recommendation to all employers is to follow the same path. Once an employee is let go, no good can come from letting him stay on and work for the rest of the day or the rest of the week. The risk is too great. I always make sure that his computer is locked while we're in the termination room, that his passwords are changed and access is denied, and that cellphones and laptops are secured.

## THE DREADED 30-SECOND HIKE

When I see the employee walk toward the conference room, then I experience what is, in my mind, the most uncomfortable 30-second hike—it's that lonely walk into the conference room for the moment that I've been dreading for a while. My heart is always pounding. No matter who the employee is or how long he's been with the firm, I always have anxiety going into the room.

But I'm a big believer that it's our job as good business owners to overcome that anxiety and make the move that we have already decided, from a rational place.

After I make the dreaded 30-second hike, I enter the conference room. Inside the room, there are six steps to completing the task of terminating an employee:

1. *Expectations.* When I enter the room, I expect to see the second person already sitting at the table with a pen and a notepad. That second person already knows what I'm going to say, but he has specific orders to not talk unless it's absolutely necessary.

   Sometimes the second person is a human resources person, and it may be fine for this person to talk to the employee. But often the second person is a manager or a trusted employee who the person being terminated may lash out at, resulting in an undesirable back and forth between the two. So it's better for the second person not to speak at all, and again, when I walk into the room, what I expect to find instead is that person ready to jot down everything that's said.

2. **The first statement.** After I walk into the room, the first statement I lead with is, "We're going to have to let you go.

   When I used to watch my old boss terminate employees, he had a strategy of trying to almost cross-examine the employee he was letting go. It was almost an attempt to get the employee to admit that he had bungled a job or he hadn't done very well on a task. This just leads to the employee being very defensive and more often than not, the employee doesn't admit what the cross-examining employer wants them to. Instead, they end up in an argument that can take several minutes, which is not only wasted time, but it heightens emotions.

Instead, what I found to be much more effective is to come right out and say what's happening. "We're going to have to let you go." It's not as harsh as Donald Trump saying, "You're fired," but it is direct and to the point. The follow-up of, "Let me tell you why," really sets the stage for that brief conversation that you have with the employee.

Once you have the employee's attention, he will want to know first and foremost why this is happening. So that simple statement, "We're going to have to let you go," really sets the stage for how the termination is going to go. You've told him what's going to happen, and now you're going to tell him why. And since you've taken control from the start, more often than not, the employee will listen.

Often, I also tell the employee, "I'm happy to listen to you once I've finished," just to let him know that I am going to give him a chance to talk. At that point, I usually follow with a few generic statements. Maybe I have a report that shows that he isn't up to par with some of his coworkers in a similar situation. Or I tell him it's just not a good fit. Whatever statement or explanation you have prepared in advance, it should be as generic as possible, and it should be discussed with your human resources attorney or human resources department in advance.

Even though I tell the employee that I'm going to tell him why he's being terminated, ultimately, as the employer, it's in your best interest to give the employee as little additional information as possible. Tell him you're terminating him or letting him go, but then give as few details as possible, and be as generic as possible if you do have any discussion.

The only exception to this is when you're trying to set an example. For instance, one time I caught an employee stealing from us. I wanted her to know that I had caught her stealing, that I wasn't going to allow it, and that she was terminated, effective immediately.

Once in a while you will want to use a termination as an example for wrongdoing. But that should be saved for situations that involve stealing, fraud, or breaking of very weighty company rules.

Even in cases like this, I go through all the steps. But in cases where the employee is increasing risk by being on the job— he's stealing from you or defrauding your clients—you need to act as quickly as possible.

Ideally, you should let the person go the same day that the events are occurring or that you discover the events occurring. We had a situation where an employee just really crossed a line in the morning, so we called our human resources attorney and discussed the problem with her, and she agreed that legally we had enough information to let the employee go. That was the safest way for us to make that move and not have to do any more investigation, so we were able to let him go that same afternoon.

When you find you've got an employee who is seriously placing the company at risk, then as soon as possible, you need to clear your calendar and make the termination a top priority. Regardless of the situation, the employee is creating risk simply by being employed by you.

Again, you still need to go through all the steps, and be as professional as possible to minimize the risk of that employee coming back at you.

3.  *Let the employee talk.* Once you have said your prepared remarks, then turn the situation over to the person being terminated and give him a chance to talk. Let him tell his side of the story. One of the biggest keys to resolving the termination with as little drama as possible is for the employee to leave the room and leave the company feeling like he was heard. This is a critical piece of the process—I can't emphasize this enough.

    In my experience, a person has only so much emotional bandwidth in any given moment. He may start off crying or yelling, or he may start swearing or attacking. But whatever his reaction, remain quiet and let him have his say. Let him feel like he's being heard, and listen as compassionately as possible.

A lot of times, we business owners get in the spot that we're in because we don't listen when people tell us no. We don't listen to doubt. We don't listen to fear. We're good at just going forward, plowing through all the problems, and getting the job done.

But oftentimes, the same personality that allows us to plow through people telling us no also inhibits us from having empathy when an employee is under duress. We just don't hear it the same. We don't have the same reaction as a more naturally empathetic person would..

So as best you can, as an employer in this moment—show some empathy and really listen as much as possible. You've already made your decision. You're not going to change your mind. But you want to let the employee know that you are listening.

4. *Your reaction.* Once the employee has had his say, it's critical that you remain calm. You must detach yourself from the emotion expressed by the employee. Try to show empathy, but remember that you have made a decision to ultimately part ways with this employee. You're not trying to win an argument or prove a point. You are winning by achieving your goal of letting the employee go, even if he leaves the room feeling like he just told you off or cursed you out.

So let the employee have his say, and then try to respond in a way that acknowledges what he said but doesn't say too much in return. For example, a statement like, "Thanks for letting us know what we could have done better. We'll make a note of that for next time. Unfortunately, we've made our decision in this situation," lets the employee know that you have listened but your decision is final.

The best way to be prepared for the employee's reply is to work out some scripted responses in advance, and then clarify those answers in your mind. See the list at the end of chapter 5. Examples are: "This isn't a good fit," or "Your performance isn't what we are looking for," or "We need more results from your position," or "Your production isn't at the same level as your coworkers," and "Our decision is final." This can help you keep from blurting out something like, "Because you have no skills." My old boss said this, and it just created unnecessary resentment and embarrassment for the employee. And for the employee, that was probably horrible to hear. The reality is she probably did have skills in several areas, just not for the task that we had assigned her.

So avoid blurting out statements that aren't thought through. It can be really helpful to have at least a generic statement as to why this isn't working. "Your numbers are down," or "You're not picking up the new tasks quickly"—anything that gives the employee something to think about. Then, later, when the employee has found a different job, instead of thinking back to what a jerk his old boss was, he may decide that his old boss was right and that his previous job wasn't a good fit and he can be happier to be in a position better suited to his skill sets.

5. *Let the emotions settle.* Immediately following the termination discussion, I let the employee stay in the room for as long

as he needs to let his emotions settle down. As I said, a person only has so much emotional bandwidth in any given situation. So no matter how much drama there was, at some point, that energy runs out. The idea for the employer, as a business owner, is to minimize any disruption to the business. So the more emotional response you can keep in the room, the better. Again, I like to have tissues on hand for this purpose.

At some point, as a business owner, I often say something like, "Well, it feels like we've said everything we have to say, but I can tell you're still feeling kind of emotional. Why don't I leave, and you sit here as long as you need with our human resources person. You can calm down and gather yourself, and if there's anything more you want to tell me, then let our human resources person know and she can get me. Otherwise, you're free to just sit here in silence, until you feel ready to leave the room," at which point I leave the room.

Since the business owner usually has a more dominating personality, sometimes leaving the room can help the person relax. Some business owners aren't comfortable leaving the room and leaving the terminated employee alone with the human resources person or someone else. But the goal is to lessen the impact on the rest of the business by letting the person calm down in the room, even if you, the business owner, have to stay in the room with him.

For me personally, knowing that it could be some time, I usually leave the room and let the person sit as long as he needs to calm down. The second person that's in the room with me has already been prepared and trained to grab me if the outgoing employee makes an inappropriate statement, starts to make a scene, or does something else that requires my attention.

6.  *The next ten minutes.* If the former employee doesn't need to sit for a while, or I'm no longer needed in the room, then the termination in the room ends with me telling the employee how the next ten minutes are going to play out.

    I usually tell the former employee, "We don't want a scene, and we also don't want you to feel embarrassed. We'd like for you to just gather your things and leave as discreetly as possible." I tell the employee this so that he can start to get a picture of how the rest of the process is going to go.

    Many people are embarrassed easily, and now his coworkers will be watching him pack up his things. So you may also want to give the employee the option of just walking out the door and then sending his belongings to him.

    Before allowing him to leave the room, you need to discuss any items the company needs to collect from the former employee—for example, keys, cellphones, laptops, or parking passes—and how the company will get those items back. Any outstanding expenses also need to be discussed at this time.

    Expanding on the discussion in chapter 3, if a severance package is part of the termination, the details of that package should be spelled out in a separation agreement, which you need to have the employee sign. When presenting the agreement, remind the former employee that the reason he's being let go is because it's not a good fit, let him know the offer the agreement contains, and then ask for his signature on the release. You should also offer this release if you feel there's a risk involved with the termination.

Again, have your human resources attorney review the release as part of the preparation for the termination to ensure it accommodates the employee's rights—for example, by state law, do you need to offer the employee a few days to review the release before signing?

## LEAVING THE TERMINATION ROOM

With the conversation over, emotions calmed, company belongings collected, and if needed, paperwork signed, everyone leaves the room. As I mentioned earlier, I'm usually not part of this process, but I encourage business leaders to participate in this part of the process until you feel comfortable passing it off to someone else.

As I said, I really encourage you to let the person know this isn't just about the company—it's also about him. One way to handle this is to tell the former employee something like, "I don't want you to feel embarrassed, but I also don't want a scene. I'm going to go with you to collect your belongings because I can't just let you be at your desk and have access to your computer and workstation unsupervised."

Even if you feel the employee doesn't have access to sensitive information, I recommend that you have eyes on the former employee at all times until he's left your premises.

I, or the other person who was in the room, walk with the employee to his desk. Whoever walks the employee to his desk then hangs back about 10 to 15 feet in a place where he can see everything the employee is doing, while not looming over him. I might even pull out my smartphone and check my email, but I'm really there to oversee him in the least intrusive way possible.

The highest risk of a disturbance in the workspace is when the former employee is at his desk gathering his belongings. If he happens to have a question while he's at his desk, I invite him back into the conference room. I just try and encourage him in a way that's commanding without being disrespectful to guide him out of the office.

Of course, if you do fear that an employee you are terminating could become violent, you should have some form of security ready or someone primed to call 911, if needed. Chances are, if you've done the last few steps correctly and allowed the person to express the emotions that he had and truly listened to him, then he's likely not going to feel like he needs to make a scene.

I have let dozens of people go in my career, and I haven't had anyone make a scene at their desk in years.

So the goal is to have the person gather his things quickly and then escort him to the door. Once he's out the door, I advise the receptionist to email everyone in the company that he is no longer an employee of the firm so that everyone knows to not let him back on the premises.

# Chapter 5 Takeaways

Five Generic Statements

1. This isn't a good fit.

2. Your performance isn't what we are looking for.

3. We need more results from your position.

4. Your production isn't at the same level as your coworkers.

5. Our decision is final.

# CHAPTER
# 6

## AFTER THE TERMINATION: NOW WHAT?

You've just completed the dramatic act of terminating an employee. Part of you is feeling better because it was probably a pretty hard task for you as a business owner. It's always hard for me, but as I've said, I feel some relief that it's over.

Just as you should be prepared before you go into the termination room and for what's going to happen with the employee after the act, you should also be prepared for how to deal with others in the organization in the aftermath.

Now is the time to remember that you are the leader. No one is a better leader than you. What your team really needs is for you to present some sort of strategy. If you present a strategy, your team will quickly follow it.

Coming up with a loose strategy in advance can go a long way in restoring confidence in you as the person who is going to resolve whatever the fallout is.

Depending on the person terminated, part of the strategy will involve planning the conversation you'll have with other members of your organization about why the termination occurred. In this meeting, you'll need to balance your reasons for letting the person go (without saying too much) with giving the remaining employees some assurances that they are somehow different from the person you let go. A little later on in this chapter, I'll give some different examples of when you'll want to have this meeting.

Most of the time, I advocate saying nothing or saying very little about the reasons for letting someone go. When it's necessary to inform the team about why the person was let go, you always need to be very careful about what you say. In my opinion, it's almost always best to be absolutely as generic and basic as possible without saying too much. It's called *coach speak* in sports, and it involves statements like, "It wasn't a good fit," or "Unfortunately, we had to go in a different direction." What you say to explain the situation is about managing risk and protecting yourself from repercussions. I'll discuss this more in depth later in this chapter.

Another point to make when you're talking to the former employee's coworkers is to remind them of some of their obligations. Many of them won't be in the mood for this conversation, and many will seemingly not hear what you say, but in time, it will resonate with them.

It's also important to stress where calls about the terminated employee should be directed—for example, to human resources or to you. In our firm, I give strict orders that no one else in our company can give references. The reason is that others in the firm typically only know enough to get us in trouble and not enough to tell the whole picture. When you let someone go, you might decide to ask them to resign, you might decide to outright fire them, or you might be laying them off because you don't have enough work. The coworkers don't really know the specifics of that conversation, and they don't need to know the specifics of that conversation. But there's always a risk that they're going to end up commenting on the details of the separation to a potential future employer, and that's something you don't want to happen.

We had a situation some years ago where we let an employee go who just wasn't good at his job, and everyone knew it. The decision to let him go was the correct one, and everyone also knew that. But to protect ourselves, we framed the decision by asking him to resign, and that's how the termination agreement was worded. If a future employer called, we'd say he resigned.

However, one manager working with us for several years, knew several people in the industry. Unbeknownst to me, a potential employer called him instead of me, and rather than referring that call to me, the manager working with us told the potential employer that we had fired the former employee.

Luckily, we didn't get into too much trouble over that statement, but it really scared me. I had a very stern conversation with that manager at the time, and I also implemented the rule that all references for jobs needed to be referred to an owner or the human resources department. That practice protects you when you fire people, because those people who have left your company are now looking for jobs in your market.

In the aftermath, you will likely have a group of employees with varying degrees of anxiety about the fact that they just saw, in essence, their own mortality. One of their coworkers was let go, which is a reminder that they could also be let go. They may be staring at you, the leader, and thinking, "Now what? What's the next step? How do we get through this? So we decided to lose this person, but how do we move the business forward?"

There are usually three groups of employees that you, the business owner, should expect to deal with in the aftermath of a termination. Not every employee on your staff will fit into one of these groups. But you should be prepared to deal with these groups.

## Group 1
## The Coworkers of the Terminated Employee

The first group is the coworkers of the individual who was terminated. These are the people in that particular department or division of your company who all share in the same work as the person who was terminated. There are two key pieces in dealing with this group: handling the anxiety and emotions and redistributing the workload.

Immediately following a termination, you will likely need to deal with the anxiety many of the former employee's coworkers will feel in the wake of the act. To help dispel those emotions, I like to bring that group of coworkers together as quickly as possible. So within 30 minutes of letting somebody go, or first thing the following morning if the termination occurred late the previous day, I bring them together to address the workflow situation and their own futures with the company.

The group may assume that some of the former employee's work will now fall back on them. They will be wondering what the next steps are to move the company forward.

The way I deal with this situation is to create a strategy in advance for those immediate coworkers and the workload. Previously in the book, we discussed the importance of timing when letting someone go, so this piece—a strategy for distributing the workload—should factor into the decision about the best time to do the termination. As part of the plan for timing the act, you should prepare a written outline of a strategy for how you are replacing the person and his work efforts.

I create that strategy by writing out all the factors I can think of that are going to affect the terminated person's team in his absence.

Included in this strategy are how I'm going to explain the termination, how I'm going to replace the terminated person, and how the timing of that will affect the team. For example, as I discussed earlier, when do you post an ad to find the replacement? Do you post that ad in advance of the termination and then have a replacement ready to show up the next business day? While that makes a lot of business sense and includes almost no downtime in manpower, it may seem cold and callous to the former employee's coworkers.

If you wait until after the termination and then post an ad, you can tell the former employee's coworkers that you didn't really want to do the termination, but you had no choice, and so you don't have a replacement prepared to step right in. This may seem like a more humane way to handle terminating an employee, but it means you could be looking at two or more weeks before there's a replacement. Is your team prepared to take on the tasks of the former employee for that length of time?

To try to determine the best answers to the many questions that come with terminating an employee, as part of the written strategy, I create a time line for the process. For example, the termination occurs at 3 p.m., I meet with the former employee's coworkers at 3:30 p.m., and one week later the replacement employee starts work. During that interim week, we're going to move a designated employee in to help with the workload, and we're going to ask everyone else to pitch in. When the replacement arrives, another designated person is going to train him. Within three weeks, we'll be up to speed.

Here are a couple of ways I handled difficult terminations when talking to the coworkers of the terminated employee:

## Challenging Termination Example 1
## Something Has Changed

One very challenging termination was letting go of one of the attorneys in the firm who had been with us for a number of years and who was on friendly terms with others in the firm. He had been to the other attorneys' homes. He had been to birthday parties. So even though it was a tough event for me to go through personally, I knew it would be even harder on his coworkers.

I wrote down all my points as part of my strategy and gathered the remaining attorneys in a room as soon as the former employee had left the building. I told the group that it was unfortunate that we had to go through this and that I understood it was emotional and difficult for them. But I told them we felt like we had to do it and that we had no choice. And one of the reasons we had no choice was because he just wasn't carrying his weight. He wasn't working as much as the rest of the team and they all knew it.

My goal was to swing the reasoning back to how the people in that room were somehow different from him, to alleviate their anxiety and assure them that they weren't going to be next just because they were a coworker or a friend.

Other than that, I gave few details because I was already very concerned about the impact of his departure on business and because I felt that with this high-ranking, long-term employee, the less said the better, other than to assure the others that he was different from them.

I also decided to humanize the act by not running an ad in advance or having a replacement already selected. So I had to inform that group of attorneys that it would be several weeks before the replacement was hired, and in the interim, I would pitch in because it was vital that we cover his work.

I explained to the group which tasks I would take on, and I went around the room and assigned each person their own two tasks. We were able to distribute his work evenly, adding a little more to each person's workload but not overburdening any one person. It ended up working out, and we had a new attorney hired and up to speed within about four weeks.

## Challenging Termination Example 2
## Downsizing

Another difficult termination was when we were actually doing a little downsizing. We had to let some key people go because we just didn't need that much staff. Often, with downsizing, you end up eliminating some people who haven't necessarily done anything to deserve termination, but it may be that they have a big salary that you can no longer afford or a big role that you no longer need.

During one of our downsizings, we let two attorneys go who had very good track records with the firm, and I knew it would be dramatic and scary for the other attorneys. I gathered the remaining attorneys in a room and I explained to them that we had to do some downsizing, and we chose two people. In this instance, I told them why we made the choices we did, which was because those two attorneys didn't offer what we needed to grow the company and to get some business back that we had lost.

Then I tried to give those attorneys in the room a couple of nuggets that they could focus on that would relieve their anxiety and potentially help them in the long run.

I also assured them that this was indeed a downsizing, so we were not hiring anyone to replace the two who we had let go. As further proof to the attorneys that they were still needed, I reassigned the work from the two terminated attorneys, and I took on some of the work myself. I think that, as a business owner, it's really key to always set the example that you are willing to do any task in your company. When you're selling really horrible news to everyone, you're also showing that you're willing to be a recipient of the bad side of that event—you're not just sitting in a lofty office, receiving a bigger profit while the others in your company get a worse job.

While I thought that was an important point to make, I was also sure the news and the extra workload was tough on them; after all, their workload went up even though their pay was staying the same. I tried to lessen the blow by reminding them that the good news was they all still had jobs. But all in all, it was a really tough conversation. Ultimately, I was quick and honest about it because the goal as the business owner at this point is to get your company functioning at normal capacity, or even better, as quickly as possible.

# Group 2
## The Unintended Witnesses

The second group of employees who you may deal with in the aftermath of a general termination is those who unintentionally witnessed the actual event (the conversation in the conference room) or who watched the terminated employee gather his belongings from his desk and exit the office. This group is different from the people what you intentionally did have witness the termination process. During the walk out, there are often several employees sitting within a few feet watching the events unfold. They're witnessing a dramatic piece of the termination, which is the person leaving.

With this group, it's important to be careful with what you say and how you move forward. In general, if it's just a classic, standard termination, I prefer to present myself as stoic as possible and go back to work as quickly as possible to set the example that we are returning to work, that we're functioning normally, and that everyone else should follow suit.

Generally, I don't comment on the termination, and I don't meet with these people. I just try to express a level of normal calmness and return to work. Although they may have some initial emotional responses, I have seen that, generally, they return to work relatively quickly.

An exception to this practice is when an employee has stolen from you or has been a part of some bad behavior that his coworkers potentially knew about.

In an instance like this, you'll want to make an example of this employee.

Earlier, I gave the example of the employee who was stealing from the company. No one ever told us, so we were paying out for over a year until we finally caught her.

When we let her go, I did not let someone else walk her to her desk and stand back while she cleaned it out. Instead, I walked her to her desk, and I hovered right over her shoulder. I was trying to set an example to her coworkers that I was very upset and that I wasn't going to tolerate this behavior. I was setting an example that it was going to be very embarrassing if you steal from the firm.

The next day, I really made a scene over the whole affair. I started the day by calling together all her coworkers and letting them know that I was upset, that I wasn't going to tolerate theft, and that I had certain expectations of them. During the rest of the day, I'd go to her desk, pull out uncompleted tasks, and vocalize to other managers how appalling it was that she'd been hiding work and that much of it hadn't been done.

I knew I was being disruptive, and in the short-term, it was counterintuitive, but I wanted to cause her coworkers who knew about the offense and didn't report it to either quit or to decide to work through my frustrations and start afresh.

In that instance, I really made quite a scene, but generally I try to return to normalcy as quickly as possible.

Reinforcing an earlier point: If you're a business owner like me who's gotten to where he is by not really listening to others—including when they respond emotionally to a situation—then you may want to balance yourself out with other designated people in the office who are better listeners, who are more approachable, and who deal much better with emotional responses by conveying empathy. Then let it be known that it's okay for employees, if they are very upset about someone being let go, to approach that designated person or persons with questions about the termination.

# Group 3
# The Gossipers

The third group of people you may have to deal with following a termination is the most dangerous group—the gossipers. This is a group of people who weren't witnesses to the act and don't have real knowledge of what happened, but for whatever reason they have decided to speculate on why the termination happened and tell others that they know why it happened.

This group usually includes people in your organization who are insecure about their own role in the company, are trying to make themselves feel better, or are trying to be liked by others by having an inside scoop on what the company is doing.

Having a group like this is often the fallout for making the decision to not give any details to coworkers on why somebody was let go.

Still, I think the safest and best move is to give as little detail as possible to the coworkers about why somebody is let go. It protects you, it limits your risk, and it's also the most respectful way to treat someone who's been let go.

In the long run, good employees wind up respecting you more for staying quiet about people who are no longer with you. But the fallout is that a percentage of employees will become those dangerous gossipers who make up the reason why this person has been let go and then tell others why they think it happened.

## MANAGING RISK IN THE WAKE OF THE TERMINATION

There are a number of risks that can occur in the wake of a termination. One is the risk of coworkers and other workers feeling somehow betrayed by the process and enough so that they either turn into bad employees, or they quit. So as much as possible, you want to avoid alienating other workers. That's why, while most of the time you want to give as few details as possible about a termination, there are times when it's important to let others know why the act occurred. Usually, these are instances when you want to make an example of an employee.

One of these I mentioned previously, which is when someone, especially a company manager, has been stealing from you.

I ended up explaining the details of that to several coworkers so that they could tell others why somebody would suddenly be fired who otherwise was doing their job. When necessary, you do want to share details to minimize the risk of alienating other good workers.

Obviously, one of the biggest risks of terminating someone is that the employee you just let go will come back and sue you. To protect yourself, let me advise once again that you should consult your human resources attorney or your human resources department, and have a good, solid basis of data to support the decision going into the termination.

That's why it's important to be very careful what is said in the aftermath. In my experience, it helps minimize the risk of a lawsuit to remain quiet and to not say anything. If you tell a roomful of five or ten employees why you let somebody go, you've just created five or ten potential witnesses that can all be deposed and used in a trial against you on this termination. That is a very scary thought as a business owner.

It's difficult to comprehend the events that are going to occur post termination. And it can be a somewhat nerve-racking emotional event that can catch you off-guard when you're going into a roomful of coworkers of the person you just let go. You have to look those people in the eye and give them your strategy and your moving-forward speech. There might even be a few people crying, and there might be a few people who are visibly angry or expressing real surprise.

Even if there are people in the group who support your decision, their reaction may be somewhat emotional in that immediate meeting. That's why, again, I like to have my strategy, my thoughts, and my action plan written out. You have to remember that your goal to make money will only be realized if this group gets back to normalcy as quickly as possible.

It's often tempting to provide all the reasons as to why you're not the villian, and that you were fair in terminating the former employee. But unless you're making a really clear example of somebody, there should be very few instances when you disclose any details. Leave the people who weren't in the termination room completely out of the situation.

I remember working for my old boss, and there was an accountant who I really liked, and he really seemed smart. He came to work every day and got his job done. One day, my old boss let him go and I could not understand why.

It wasn't until a couple of years later when I bought out my old boss and started running the company that I actually learned that there was actually a legitimate reason for letting the accountant go.

I didn't find out the truth until years later because there were actions in place to protect me from it, and as a good worker, I just wanted to get back to my normal life. That's one reason I believe that good workers like to just get back to normal life as soon as possible. Even though I didn't know the details, and even though on the surface I didn't agree with the decision, I just returned to my normal working life.

In my experience, every company that is really successful—regardless of the company's size—has a good system in place for terminating people, while every company that I know that is failing struggles at letting people go.

Business is an ever-evolving animal, and business success constantly ebbs and flows. Any company that is fortunate enough to stay in business for some time will likely go through periods of downsizing. Even if your company is one that is really well run and making money and has a good client base, you're still likely to have times where you'll have to do some downsizing.

The key differentiator between companies that stay around for a long time and companies that really struggle or go under is that those that stay in business are better at controlling costs. The best way to control costs is to control payroll.

So whether it's an employee who is being overpaid for his production or one employee who is really disruptive and causing others around him to lose production, or you simply need to do some downsizing of duplicate positions, controlling your payroll costs by letting people go in a humane and efficient way is going to help your company achieve its goals and stay healthy and strong in the long term.

I hope you've found some good tips and takeaways from reading about my system. Even though it's a challenge to deal with letting an underperforming or disruptive employee go, as a business owner, it is our obligation to remove those people from the business. To not do so is a disservice to your business, your profits, and to all those other employees who are trying to make a better life for themselves through the opportunity you're giving them.

# Chapter 6 Takeaways

1} Stick to generic *coach speak* and be as basic as possible with statements like, "It wasn't a good fit," or "Unfortunately, we had to go in a different direction."

2} There are three groups of employees who you may need to deal with in the aftermath:

- The coworkers: These are the people who worked with the employee. You may need to have a brief talk with these people to re-distribute workflow and get them back to normal.

- The witnesses: These are the people who worked in the near vicinity of the employee and watched him clean out his desk and be escorted off the property. The less said the better to these employees.

- The gossipers: This is the group that doesn't know what really happened and makes up its own story about the event. The less said the better with this group.

# APPENDIX

## SANDWICH PRODUCTION
### PER HOUR

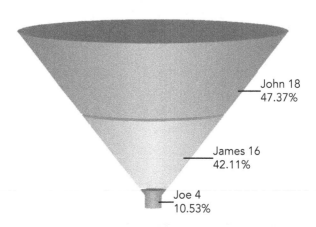

John 18
47.37%

James 16
42.11%

Joe 4
10.53%

Example A

| SANDWICH | TIME | USER |
|----------|------|------|
| Tuna | 12:02 | James |
| BLT | 12:09 | James |
| BLT | 12:10 | James |
| BLT | 12:13 | James |
| Ham | 12:15 | James |
| Tuna | 12:20 | James |
| PB&J | 12:24 | James |
| PB&J | 12:25 | James |
| Tuna | 12:27 | James |
| Ham | 12:31 | James |
| Tuna | 12:33 | James |

| | | |
|---|---|---|
| BLT | 12:35 | James |
| Ham | 12:37 | James |
| Ham | 12:41 | James |
| Tuna | 12:44 | James |
| BLT | 12:51 | James |
| Ham | 12:02 | Joe |
| BLT | 12:17 | Joe |

Example B

| Date/Day | Number of Violations | Number of Sandwiches Produced | Comments |
|---|---|---|---|
| Monday | 3 | 13 | late for work |
| Tuesday | 2 | 18 | |
| Wednesday | 0 | 14 | |
| Thursday | 0 | 19 | |
| Friday | 1 | 17 | late for work |

| Ideal Qualities For POsition | Actual Abilities |
|---|---|
| Hard working, always on time, positive attitude | Struggles to be on time. Sometimes has a negative attitude. |
| Skilled at making sandwiches with a smile and greeting customers | Not as friendly as I would like. |
| Produces at least 25 sandwiches per hour of employment | Has never produced 25 sandwiches in an hour. |
| Eager to take on new tasks when store is slow | I have to constantly ask if Jim is available for other tasks. |

Example C

# ABOUT THE AUTHOR

Isaac Hammer is the co-owner of a creditors' rights law firm in Seattle. Three years after graduating from law school, Hammer and his attorney wife, Karen, purchased the firm they were working for and grew it from five attorneys and more than two dozen employees to 15 attorneys and more than 100 employees operating in seven states.

Today, the firm's clients include most of the Fortune 100 banks and some of the top brands in the world.

The firm has grown through acquisition and by taking advantage of opportunities in other markets.

Hammer has developed his own methods for terminating people, having been in the position to let employees go numerous times because they were no longer a good fit, couldn't keep up with the speed of growth of the company, or because they were in duplicate roles.

Printed in the USA
CPSIA information can be obtained
at www.ICGtesting.com
JSHW011403010724
65696JS00019B/670